SELECTIONS
from the
WRITINGS
of
FÉNELON

SELECTIONS
from the
WRITINGS
of
FÉNELON

WHITAKER
HOUSE

SELECTIONS FROM THE WRITINGS OF FÉNELON:
With a Memoir of His Life

ISBN: 978-1-62911-015-8
eBook ISBN: 978-1-62911-039-4
Printed in the United States of America
© 2014 by Whitaker House

Whitaker House
1030 Hunt Valley Circle
New Kensington, PA 15068
www.whitakerhouse.com

1 2 3 4 5 6 7 8 9 10 11   21 20 19 18 17 16 15 14

PREFACE

No apology is necessary for giving anything to the public from the pen of Fénelon. Such were the elevation and liberality of his spirit, that it soared above party to diffuse itself over all the interests of humanity.

He was, in spirit and in truth, a Christian—a lover of God and man. His pure and expansive thoughts could not in their nature be confined to any sect or country. It is true that he was not above all the prejudices and influences of education. Who is? But his was one of those pure and beneficent spirits that, from their natures, belong to the whole of mankind.

It is not contended that he has done as much as some others to enlarge the limits of human science. His political maxims were just and pure, and they were fearlessly promulgated at the expense of his highest temporal interests. And it is scarcely worth considering whether he was as well acquainted with all the rules of political economy as others, whose residence and situation gave them greater advantages in that respect. It is not as a politician, but as a Christian and a man, that we regard his character.

Fénelon was born and brought up a Roman Catholic. He was a dignitary in that arbitrary and exclusive church. It was not possible that his thoughts and feelings should not be affected by this circumstance. What we have to wonder and rejoice at is that his pure and expansive affections burst all exclusive bands. His heart belonged to no creed and no country but embraced the earth and soared to heaven. He loved all that was lovely on earth, and his aspirations were to all that is elevated above it.

This putting forth of the affections from and above himself was the ennobling and distinctive trait in the character of Fénelon. He loved men, not because they were of the same race but because they were susceptible of virtue and happiness. He loved God, not merely as his benefactor but as the great source of felicity to all sentient existence.

Fénelon was pious—pious in the highest sense of the term. He did not submit to commands because the lawgiver was powerful and could punish disobedience or because he was just and his commands equitable. Rather, his spirit voluntarily went forth to cooperate in all the designs of goodness. His efforts were never retarded or interrupted. He threw off, if he ever felt them, the bonds of indolence, and the mists of selfishness never impaired his vision. The pure and holy influences of such a spirit should surely be diffused as widely as possible, and this is the design of the present volume.

The direct influence of such a mind ought not to be confined to those who have acquired a foreign language and can afford to purchase books extensively. It is not invidious to say that there is no existing translation of Fénelon's works that renders this volume unnecessary. To render the work as cheap and easily attainable as possible, it is confined to a few selections. The translation is a free one, but sedulous care has been taken never to depart from the spirit of the author nor to introduce any but his ideas. As the productions of a Roman Catholic and one zealously attached to his church, his writings necessarily contain many things that could not be acceptable to Christians of all denominations. These have been uniformly omitted. The translator has no other ambition than to render the rich treasures of the mind and heart of Fénelon accessible to those of another age and country—or any other wish than that the reader may imbibe something of the spirit of the author.

CONTENTS

I

MEMOIR OF FÉNELON[1]

---

1. This Memoir is intended to contain all the interesting facts relating to the life of Fénelon. It has been compiled from various authors, whose own words have been retained wherever it seemed expedient.

Poche menti vegg'io ricche di lume;
  E quelle poche oscura orgoglio altero:
  Luminoso intelletto, e umil pensiero
  Di star concordi insiem non han costume.

Sallo per suo dolor l'Angiol primiero,
  Che sì fulgido uscì di man del Nume;
  Ah! spiegherebbe in ciel le aurate piume,
  Se non torcea superbia il lor sentiero.

Quindi in quest' Angiol novo io non ammiro
  L'ampio saper, che folgorando ascende
  Per le vie della terra e dell' empiro:

Allor l'ammiro, quando in sè discende,
  E quel che gli orna il crin fulgido giro
  A sè lo toglie, e al Donator lo rende.

                                        —Sappa

A mind full fraught with intellectual light,
Is rarely found; and oft when found, its beams,
Obscured by pride, emit but shadowy gleams:
Humility scarce dwells with genius bright.

The first and brightest of the angel host,
Son of the Morning! still in heaven he might
On golden pinions bear his upward flight,
Had not his glorious state by pride been lost.

Hence this new Angel, my admiring eye
Follows with far less rapture when he soars,
In intellectual greatness rising high,
And, like the lightning, heaven and earth explores,
Than when from his own brow he takes the golden crown,
And at his feet, who gave it, humbly lays it down.

                                        —Nat. Gaz.

François de Salignac de la Mothe-Fénelon was born at the castle of Fénelon, in Perigord, on the sixth day of August 1651. His family has derived more luster from the single name of the Archbishop of Cambrai than from a long series of ancestors who filled the most distinguished stations in the cabinet, in the field, and in the church.

Fénelon was brought up under the paternal roof until his twelfth year, for his constitution was very weak and delicate. This circumstance, added to his amiable disposition, made him an object of peculiar tenderness to his father. There was nothing remarkable attending his early education; it was entrusted to a preceptor, who appears to have possessed the principles of sound literature and who knew how to render it acceptable to his pupil. He gave him in a few years a more extensive knowledge of the Greek and Latin languages than is usually obtained at so early an age.

When he was twelve years old, Fénelon was sent to the University of Cahors, not far removed from the residence of his family. He there completed his philosophical and philological studies, and he even took the degrees that were afterward of sufficient efficacy when he was elevated to ecclesiastical dignities. The Marquis Antoine de Fénelon, his uncle, interested by what he heard of his young nephew, sent for him to come to Paris and placed him at the college of Plessis, where he continued his philosophical studies and also commenced those of theology. It was there he formed a friendship with the young Abbé de Noailles, who was afterward the cardinal and archbishop of Paris.

The young Abbé de Fénelon distinguished himself so much at the college of Plessis that they allowed him to preach at the age of fifteen; his sermon was an extraordinary success. A similar circumstance is related of Bossuet, who at the same age preached before the most brilliant assembly in Paris with the same applause. It is curious to remark this coincidence of opinion, so prematurely formed of two men who were both destined to be the instructors of princes and to become the ornament and glory of the French church.

The Marquis de Fénelon was rather alarmed than gratified by the encomiums bestowed upon his nephew. Some idea of the frankness and austerity of his character may be formed from what he said to M. de Harlay upon his nomination to the archbishopric of Paris. "There is, sir," said he, "a great difference between the day when such a nomination procures you the compliments of all France, and the day of your death, when you will appear before God to render Him an account of your office." He had lost his only son at the siege of Candia and had found in religion the only support that could uphold his courage under so severe an affliction.

Such was the man who acted as the father and guide of Fénelon in the path of virtue and honor. Providence treasured up for the Marquis de Fénelon the most lenient of all consolations in replacing the son he had lost by a nephew, who became the object of his most tender care and affection. This nephew the Marquis hastened to secure from the snares of a deceitful world by placing him at the seminary of Saint Sulpice under the direction of M. Tronson, there to acquire a just knowledge of himself.

It was from the erudition, the example, and the tender and affectionate piety of this excellent man that the youthful Fénelon derived his relish for virtue and religion, which made him so perfect a model of excellence in all those various employments with which he was entrusted and those elevated functions that he discharged. It was about this time that Fénelon is supposed to have contemplated devoting himself to the mission of Canada, as the congregation of Saint Sulpice had a considerable establishment at Montreal; but his uncle was justly alarmed at the project, which was incompatible with the delicate constitution of his nephew, and he refused his permission. He accordingly, after having been ordained at Saint Sulpice, devoted himself to the functions of his holy office in the same parish.

It was during the exercise of this ministry that Fénelon—by mixing with all ranks and conditions, by associating with the unfortunate and the sorrowful, by assisting the weak, and by that union of mildness, energy, and benevolence that adapts itself to every character and to every situation—acquired the knowledge of the moral and physical ills that afflict human nature. It was by this habitual and immediate communication with all classes of society that he obtained the melancholy conviction of the miseries that distress the greater part of mankind. And to the profound impression of this truth through his whole life, we must ascribe that tender commiseration for the unfortunate, which he manifests in all his writings and which he displayed still more powerfully in all his actions.

He devoted himself for three years to the ecclesiastical ministry, and at the end of that time, he was appointed, by the curate of the parish of Saint Sulpice, to explain the Sacred Writings to the people on Sundays and on festival days—an office that first introduced him to public notice and from which he derived the greatest personal advantages.

Fénelon resumed, in 1674, his project of becoming a missionary, but, being convinced that his health would not sustain the rigor of a Canadian climate, he directed his thoughts to the Levant. We have a proof of this intention in a letter written by him, dated at Sarlat, the residence of his uncle, where he was upon a visit. It is so remarkable that we have thought it worthy of transcription.

> Several trifling events have hitherto prevented my return to Paris, but I will at length set out, sir, and I will almost fly thither. But compared to this journey, I meditate a much greater one. The whole of Greece opens before me, and the Sultan flies in terror; the Peloponnesus breathes again in liberty, and the church of Corinth will flourish once more; the voice of the apostle will be heard there again. I seem to be transported among those enchanting places and those precious ruins where, while I collect the most curious relics of antiquity, I imbibe also its spirit. I seek for the Areopagus, where Saint Paul declared to the sages of the world the unknown God! But next to what is sacred, I am delighted with what is profane, and I disdain not to descend to the Piraeus, where Socrates drew up the plan

of his Republic. I reach the double summit of Parnassus; I pluck the laurels of Delphi; revel in the charms of Tempe.

When will the blood of the Turks mingle with that of the Persians on the plains of Marathon and leave the whole of Greece to religion, to philosophy, and the fine arts, who regard her as their country.

> "Arva, beata
> Petamus arva, divites et insulas."

Nor will I forget thee, oh thou happy island, consecrated by the celestial visions of the well beloved disciple. Oh happy Patmos! I will kneel upon the earth and kiss the steps of the apostle, and I will believe that the heavens open on my sight. I behold the downfall of schism and the union of the East and West and the dayspring again dawning in Asia after a night of such long darkness. I behold the land that has been sanctified by the steps of Jesus and watered by His blood, delivered from its profanation and clothed anew in glory, and I behold also the children of Abraham, scattered over the face of the globe, and more numerous than the stars of heaven, assembled from the four quarters of the earth, coming to acknowledge Christ whom they pierced and to show the resurrection to the end of time.

This is enough, sir, and you will probably be glad to learn that this is my last letter and the end of my enthusiasm, which has perhaps wearied you. Excuse the eagerness that prompts me to discourse with you at a distance while waiting till I can do it in person.

—François de Fénelon

We perceive from the tone and style of this letter that it was written during that youthful period of life when the untamed imagination delights to decorate what it contemplates and to scatter forth its brightest hues. It was probably addressed to Bossuet.

Fénelon, it appears, succeeded in obtaining the consent of his uncle to his going as a missionary to the Levant, because he could not allege the same objection as the one he had against his going to Canada. There is no doubt, however, that the fear of inflicting pain upon his uncle, and subsequent reflection, made him suspend the execution of his project, and soon after, his friends succeeded in giving his zeal another direction. He was nominated by the archbishop of Paris, Superior to the society of *Nouvelles Catholiques*. It had been instituted in 1631; its object was to strengthen the faith of newly converted females and to instruct persons of the same sex who showed any desire of conversion in the doctrines of the church. Fénelon entered upon this path with pleasure, as it had some similarity with his earliest wish of becoming a missionary. It was at this time that he formed an intimacy with Bossuet, for whom he seems to have had a filial veneration.

To enable him to live in Paris, the Bishop of Sarlat, his uncle, resigned to him the priory of Carenac. This benefice, which was worth about three or four thousand livres a year, was the only one that Fénelon had until his forty-third year. For ten years, he devoted himself to the simple direction of a community of women. Some may say that such an employment, at his time of life, must have circumscribed his mind by fixing it upon uninteresting details and useless studies. It was, however, during this period when he wrote his first works, the *Treatise on the Education of Girls* and the *Treatise on the Mission of the Clergy*. The first of these was not composed for the public but for his friend the Duchess of Beauvilliers. Thus, a work that was originally intended for the use of a single family has become an elementary book equally adapted to every family and to all times and all places.

Fénelon was called at this time to mourn the death of his uncle, who had directed his first steps in the path of life and who had been still more useful to him by turning his heart toward the sublime idea of Christian perfection. It was under his eyes, in his house, and in the intimacy of that tender confidence that a father delights to show toward a favorite child, that Fénelon imbibed his unshaken conviction of the duties and greatness of his ministry.

The next event in the life of Fénelon was the choice of him by Louis XIV as a missionary to convert the Protestants of the provinces of Poitou and Saintonge. Fénelon, in an interview with the king before he set out upon his mission, refused a military escort, and when the king represented the danger he might be exposed to, he answered, "Sire, ought a missionary to fear danger? If you hope for an apostolical harvest, we must go in the true character of apostles. I would rather perish by the hands of my mistaken brethren than see one of them exposed to the inevitable violence of the military." In a letter to a duke, he said, "The work of God is not effected in the heart by force; that is not the true spirit of the gospel."

An officer in the army consulted him to know what course he should adopt with those of his soldiers who were Huguenots. Fénelon answered, "Tormenting and teasing heretic soldiers into conversion will answer no end. It will not succeed; it will only produce hypocrites. The converts so made will desert in crowds." And long afterward, when he was archbishop of Cambrai, hearing that some peasants in Hainaut who were descended from Protestants, and who held still the same opinions, had received the sacrament from a minister of their own persuasion but that, when they were discovered, they disguised their sentiments and even went to mass, he said to the reformed minister, "Brother, you see what has happened. It is full time that these good people should have some fixed religion; go and obtain their names and those of all their families. I give you my word that in less than six months they will all have passports." Fénelon received this same clergyman, whose name was Brunice, at his table as a brother and treated him with great kindness.

This was the spirit that animated Fénelon in his mission to the Protestants. Those who were not converted by him were charmed with his character; while they refused to yield to his pathetic exhortations, they never refused him their esteem and their admiration and, we may even say, their love and confidence.

The reputation that Fénelon acquired by his exertions in Poitou made him an object of public attention, and it was not long after that he was appointed preceptor to the Duke of Burgundy, the heir apparent to the kingdom. This he owed to the friendship and esteem of the Duke de Beauvilliers, who had been appointed by the king to be the governor to the young prince and who immediately named Fénelon for his preceptor. The choice of the new governor and preceptor was no sooner made public than all France resounded with applause.

The character of the Duke of Burgundy is described as violent and difficult to manage; he is said to have given indications in his earliest years of everything that was to be feared in temper and disposition. "The Duke of Burgundy," says Saint Simon, "was unfeeling and irritable to the last degree, even against inanimate objects. Passionately addicted to every kind of pleasure, he was often ferocious, naturally cruel, and inordinately proud; he looked upon men only as atoms with whom he had no sort of similarity whatever. Even his brothers scarcely seemed, in his estimation, to form an intermediate link between him and the rest of mankind. But the brilliancy of his mind and his penetration were at all times evident, and even in his moments of greatest violence, he showed proofs of genius. The extent and vigor of his mind were prodigious and prevented him from steady and direct application."

Such was the nature of the young prince confided to Fénelon. There was everything to be feared and everything to be hoped from a soul possessing such energy. From the combined efforts of those engaged in his instruction, but principally, as it seems, from the influence of the religious principle, as employed by Fénelon, the unruly and violent prince became affable, mild, humane, moderate, patient, modest, humble, and severe only toward himself. He was wholly occupied with his future obligations in life, which he felt to be great, and he thought only of uniting the duties of the son and the subject with those that he saw himself destined afterward to fulfill. But what incessant vigilance, what art, what industry, what skill, what variety in the means adopted, and what delicacy of observation must have concurred to produce such an extraordinary alteration in the character of a child, a prince, and the heir to a throne.

Fénelon composed his *Fables*, the *Dialogues of the Dead*, and *Telemachus* for the use of the prince. But, as we have before mentioned, it was by keeping alive the feeling of accountability to the King of Kings that he acquired such an influence over the mind of the high-spirited duke and succeeded in subduing his passions. He was ever presenting to him that awful day when he was to appear before the Judge of all. He strove by every means to awaken and cherish sentiments that were truly religious in the soul of his pupil and to make him feel the solemn truth that he was ever speaking and acting in the presence of God. This was the secret of the almost miraculous effect produced upon the character of the pupil of Fénelon.

During five years, Fénelon received no mark of favor from Louis XIV, and the small living bestowed upon him by his uncle was but a scanty means of support to him. He is described as being obliged to practice the most rigid economy. At last, at the age of forty-three, he was nominated to the Abbey of Saint Valéry. The king informed him of this in person and apologized for so tardy an acknowledgment of his gratitude.

His success in the education of the prince, his excellent character, and his conciliating manners had procured him the love and esteem of all who knew him, and a year after this time, he was elevated to the dignity of Archbishop of Cambrai. Fénelon showed his disinterestedness by immediately resigning the Abbey of Saint Valéry. Louis at first refused to receive his resignation, but Fénelon insisted, saying the resources of the archbishopric of Cambrai were such as made a plurality of livings against the canons of the church.

A short time previous to his nomination to the archbishopric of Cambrai, his acquaintance commenced with Madame Guyon, which was the cause of his unhappy controversy with his friend Bossuet. The doctrine of disinterested love—or that God is to be loved for His own perfections without any view to the future rewards or punishments, which was the doctrine of Fénelon—appears to have been the radical point of controversy. Those who supposed that they had attained this habitual state of divine love were called Quietists, from the perfect freedom from hope or fear that it produced. They thought that God was to be worshipped in the entire silence and stillness of the soul, in a perfect renunciation of self to Him.

Fénelon, who was one of four ecclesiastics appointed to examine this doctrine of Madame Guyon, could find nothing in it to condemn, and he even defended her as far as he could against her persecutors, who, as a result, became his enemies. When he was accused of holding doctrines contrary to the true faith and was called upon to make his defense by a declaration of his true sentiments, he published his *Explication des Maximes des Saints sur la Vie Intérieure*. Bossuet, who was entirely opposed to Fénelon upon the doctrine of disinterested love to God, used this book as a weapon against him; he accused Fénelon of fanaticism to the king. As Louis in his heart had never liked a man whose whole life and character were a tacit reproach upon his own, he readily believed all that was said against him. Thus, Fénelon was forbidden to remain in Paris, and soon after, the king, with his own hand, struck out his name as preceptor of the Duke of Burgundy.

The controversy, which was carried on with great warmth by Bossuet and supported on the part of Fénelon with great ability but with unfailing meekness, was finally submitted to the Pope and his Cardinals. The Pontiff disapproved of some propositions that were advanced by Fénelon, and the Archbishop acquiesced. The Pope is related to have made a remark respecting the controversy that could not have been very pleasing to the opponents of Fénelon. "Fénelon," he said, "was in fault for too great love of God, and his enemies were in fault for too little love of their neighbor." As a specimen of

Fénelon's style and manner of vindicating himself against the writings of Bossuet, we give the following passage.

How painful is it to me that I must carry on against you this combat of words, and that, to defend myself against your terrible charges, it should be necessary for me to point out your misrepresentations of my doctrine. I am the writer so dear to you, whom you always carry in your heart, yet you endeavor to plunge me, as another Molinos, into the gulf of Quietism. Everywhere you weep over my misfortunes, and while you weep, you tear me in pieces! What can be thought of tears to which you have recourse only for the purpose of crimination! You weep on my account, and you suppress what is essential in my writings. You join together sentences in them that are wide asunder. Your own exaggerated consequences, formally contradicted in my text, you hold out as my principles. What is most pure in my doctrine becomes blasphemy in your representation of it. Believe me, we have been too long a spectacle to the world, an object of derision to the ungodly, of compassion to the good.

That other men should be men is not surprising, but that the ministers of Jesus Christ, the angels of the church, should exhibit such scenes to the profane, to the unbeliever, calls for tears of blood. How much more fortunate would have been our lot if, instead of thus consuming our time in interminable disputes, we had been employed in our dioceses in teaching the catechism, in instructing the villager to fear God and bless His holy name.

The enemies of Fénelon finally succeeded in obtaining the condemnation of his book *Les Maximes*. It was with great reluctance that the Pope yielded at last to Fénelon's enemies; yet, in the manner in which he issued the decree, he discovered the greatest tenderness and respect for Fénelon.

This truly great man was informed that his book was condemned by the Pope just at the very moment when he was about to ascend the pulpit to preach. As deeply as he must have been affected by a decision so unexpected, yet his religion held such perfect empire over his mind that he meditated a few moments only and then, changing the entire plan of his sermon, delivered one upon perfect submission to the authority of superiors. The news of the condemnation of Fénelon had spread rapidly through the whole congregation, and this admirable presence of mind, this pious submission, this sublime tranquility, drew tears of tenderness, grief, love, and admiration from every eye. He immediately prepared his public declaration of submission to the decree of the Pope. It was simple, entire, and without any reserve. We extract from it the following passages.

> We will find consolation, my dearest brethren, in what humbles us, provided that the ministry of the Word, which we have received for your sanctification, be not enfeebled and that, notwithstanding the humiliation of the pastor, the flock will increase in grace before God....Heaven forbid that we should ever be spoken of, except to remember that a pastor thought it his duty to be more docile than the meanest sheep of his flock and that his submission was unlimited.

The submission of Fénelon was not a respectful silence, a measure of policy, or any compromise with truth; but, as he himself said to a friend, it was "an inward act of obedience rendered to God alone, according to the principles of Catholicism, I regarded the decision of my superiors as an echo of the Supreme Will. I forgot all the passions, prejudices, and disputes that preceded my condemnation; I heard God speak to me as He did to Job; I accepted my condemnation in its most extensive sense." He very justly discriminated between the meaning he intended to convey in his book and the actual sense of the text, of which he considered the Pope the infallible judge. While he still solemnly asserted that it had never been his intention to advocate those errors for which his book was condemned, the Pope's condemnation was sufficient to convince him that these errors were there expressed. And in his answer to an unknown friend who wished to write in defense of his book, he would not consent to have even his own personal intention vindicated from the errors imputed to him, lest it should appear as an indirect vindication of his book and a want of sincerity in his submission to the Pope. "In the name of God," he said, "speak to me only of God, and leave men to judge of me as they like. As to myself, I will seek only peace and silence."

Fénelon seemed not to have regarded his banishment to his diocese as any calamity, except from a fear that it might lessen his usefulness. He loved the country and rural pleasures, and he was particularly fond of walking. He wrote to a friend, "I amuse myself, I walk, and I find myself peaceful, in silence before God. Oh blissful communion! In His presence we are never alone; as to men, we are alone when we do not wish to be with them."

In the course of his walks, he would often join the peasants, sit down with them on the grass, talk with them, and console them. He visited them in their cottages, seated himself at table with them, and partook of their humble meals. By such kindness and familiarity, he won their affections and gained access to their minds. As they loved him as a father and friend, they delighted to listen to his instructions and to submit to his guidance. Long after his death, the old people who had the happiness of seeing him on these occasions spoke of him with the most tender reverence. "There," they would say, "is the chair in which our good Archbishop used to sit in the midst of us; we will see him no more," and then their tears would flow.

The diocese of Cambrai was often the theatre of war, and it experienced the cruel ravages of retreating and conquering armies. But an extraordinary respect was paid to Fénelon by the invaders of France. The English, the Germans, and the Dutch rivaled the inhabitants of Cambrai in their veneration for the Archbishop. All distinctions of religion and sect, and all feelings of hatred and jealousy that divided the nations, seemed to disappear in the presence of Fénelon. Military escorts were offered him for his personal security, but these he declined, and he traversed the countries desolated by war to visit his flock, trusting in the protection of God. In these visits, his way was marked by alms and benefactions. While he was among them, the people seemed to enjoy peace in the midst of war. He brought together into his palace the wretched inhabitants of the country whom the war had driven from their homes, and he took care of them and fed them at his own table. Seeing, one day, that one of these peasants ate nothing, he asked him the reason of his abstinence. "Alas, my lord," said the poor man, "in making my escape from my cottage, I had not time to bring off my cow, which was the support of my family. The enemy will drive her away, and I will never find another so good." Fénelon, availing himself of his privilege of safe conduct, immediately set out, accompanied by a single servant, and drove the cow back himself to the peasant.

"This," said Cardinal Maury, "is perhaps the finest act of Fénelon's life." He adds, "Alas for the man who reads it without being affected." Another anecdote showing his tenderness to the poor is thus related of him. A literary man whose library was destroyed by fire has been deservedly admired for saying, "I should have profited but little by my books, if they had not taught me how to bear the loss of them." The remark of Fénelon, who lost his in a similar way, is still more simple and touching: "I would much rather they were burnt than the cottage of a poor peasant."

The virtues of Fénelon give his history the air of romance, but his name will never die. Transports of joy were heard at Cambrai when his ashes were discovered, which, it was thought, had been scattered by the tempest of the Revolution; and to this day, the Flemings call him "the good Archbishop."

The kindness and humanity of Fénelon to the sufferers in the war endeared him to the whole nation. His charity embraced the rich and the poor, his friends and his enemies. "It is impossible," says his biographer, "to conceive how much he was the idol of the military and how Versailles, in spite of her stern master, resounded with his name. His charity and polite attentions extended equally to the prisoners of war as to his own countrymen. Virtue herself became more beautiful from Fénelon's manner of being virtuous."

One of the curates of his diocese complained to him that he was unable to put a stop to dances on the feast days.

"Mr. Curate," said Fénelon to him, "let us abstain from amusement ourselves, but let us permit these poor people to dance. Why prevent them from forgetting for a moment their poverty and wretchedness?"

The simplicity of Fénelon's character obtained for him a triumph on one occasion that must have been most gratifying to his feelings, if only as a testimony in favor of the irresistible charm and power of virtue. His enemies (for, to the reproach of human nature, Fénelon had his enemies) were mean enough to practice the shameful artifice of placing about him an ecclesiastic of high birth whom he considered only as his grand vicar but who was to act as a spy upon him. This man, who had consented to undertake so base an office, had, however, the magnanimity to punish himself for it. Subdued by the purity and gentleness of spirit that he witnessed in Fénelon, he threw himself at his feet, confessed the unworthy part he had been led to act, and withdrew from the world to conceal, in retirement, his grief and shame.

Fénelon, so indulgent of others, required no indulgence to be exercised toward him. Not only was he willing to have his failings treated with severity, but he was even grateful for it.

Father Seraphin, a Capuchin missionary of more zeal than eloquence, preached at Versailles before Louis XIV. The Abbé Fénelon, at that time the king's chaplain, being present, fell asleep. Father Seraphin perceived it and, stopping in the midst of his discourse, said, "Wake that Abbé who is asleep and who seems to be present here only to pay his court to the king." Fénelon was fond of relating this anecdote. With the truest satisfaction, he praised the preacher, who was not deterred from exercising such apostolic liberty, and the king, who approved of it by his silence.

So tender and so delicate, if the expression may be allowed, was Fénelon's love of virtue that he considered nothing as innocent that could wound it in the slightest degree. He censured Moliere for having represented it in *The Misanthrope* with an austerity that exposed it to odium and ridicule. The criticism may not be just, but we must respect the feeling that dictated it, especially because the gentle and indulgent virtue of Fénelon was far from bearing any resemblance to the savage and inflexible virtue of *The Misanthrope*. On the contrary, Fénelon relished highly *The Hypocrite* by the same author, for the more he loved genuine virtue, the more he detested the affectation of it (which he complained of meeting so often at Versailles), and the more he commended those who endeavored to expose it. He did not, like Baillet, make it a crime in Moliere to have usurped the right of the clergy to reprove hypocrites. Fénelon was persuaded that those who complain of encroachments on this right—which, after all, is only the right of every good man—are commonly slow to make use of it themselves and are even afraid to have others exercise it for them. He dared to blame Bourdaloue, whose talents and virtues he otherwise respected, for having attacked, in one of his sermons, that excellent comedy where the contrast between true and false piety is so well painted. "Bourdaloue," said he, with his usual candor, "is not a hypocrite, but his enemies will say that he is a Jesuit."

Fénelon showed his magnanimity as well as his charity during the war. He was then an exile in his own diocese and in disgrace with the king, but the enemy soldiers became his protectors and friends, and while all of France was suffering from famine, his magazines were filled with grain. He distributed it among the soldiers of his unjust master and refused to receive any pay for it, saying, "The king owes me nothing, and in times of calamity, it is my duty, as a citizen and a bishop, to give back to the state what I have received from it." It was thus that he avenged himself for his disgrace.

His mind, dead to vanity, was in conversation entirely given up to the person with whom he conversed. Men of every profession, proficient in every branch of knowledge, were at ease in his company. He directed everyone first to the subject he best understood, and then he disappeared at once, thus giving them an opportunity to produce, out of their own stock, the materials they were most able to furnish. Thus everyone parted from him well pleased with himself.

The different writings in philosophy, theology, and *belles lettres* that came from the pen of Fénelon have made his name immortal. The most powerful charm of his writings is the feeling of quiet and tranquility that they excite in the reader. It is a friend who approaches you and pours his soul into yours. You feel that you are holding an intimate communion with a pure and highly gifted mind. He moderates and suspends, at least for a while, your worldly cares and your sorrows; you enter for a time into that spirit of self-sacrifice and self-oblivion that seems to be the keynote of all his writings. Your whole heart seems to expand with the Christian love that inspired him. We are ready to forgive human nature in so many men who make us hate it, on account of Fénelon who makes us love it.

In the authors whom he quotes in his *Dialogue upon Eloquence* and *Letter to the French Academy* and cites as models, those touches of feeling that go to the soul are those upon which he loves to repose. He there seems, if we may so speak, to breathe sweetly his native air and to find himself in the midst of what is most dear to him. His sermons were always the outpourings of his heart; it was not his object to be brilliant. He retired to his oratory, and there, in the presence of God, he called up to his mind all those pure conceptions and affectionate sentiments with which his discourses were filled. Like Moses, the friend of God, he went to the holy mountain and returned to the people to communicate to them what he had learned in that ineffable communion. He would begin by instructing his flock upon the reasons of our faith and our hope and then hasten to inculcate that charity that produces and perfects all the virtues.

When the question was discussed before the Queen of Poland which of the two champions, Bossuet or Fénelon, had rendered the greatest services to religion, the Princess said, "The one has proved its truth; the other has made it to be loved." Although the spirit of love is manifest in all his writings, it is most deeply impressed on those that were composed for his pupil. He seems, in writing them, to have ever repeated to himself, "What I am going to say to this child will be the occasion of happiness or misery to twenty millions of people." He said that, not having been able to procure for the Duke of Burgundy the privilege of actually traveling himself, he had made him travel over the world with Mentor and Telemachus. "If he ever travel," added he, "I should wish that it might be without an equipage. The less retinue he had, the easier would truth be able to approach him. He would be able to see good and evil, so as to adopt the one and avoid the other, much better abroad than at home. And delivered for a while from the cares and anxieties of being a prince, he would taste the pleasure of being a man."

Let us not forget the most interesting fact relative to the education of this prince, which bound him by the strongest tie of affection to his instructor. When Fénelon committed any fault, even the slightest, in the execution of this trust, he never failed to accuse himself of it to his pupil. What an authority, founded in love and confidence, must he have acquired over him by this ingenuous frankness! What a lesson of uprightness must it have taught him—openness and ingenuousness even at the expense of his self-love, indulgence toward the faults of others, readiness to confess his own, the courage even to accuse himself, the noble ambition of knowing, and the still more noble ambition of conquering himself. "If you wish," said a philosopher, "to have your son listen to stern, unbending truth, begin by speaking it to him when it is against yourself."

The enemies of Fénelon have insinuated most falsely that he took side in the controversy against Jansenism only because the Cardinal de Noailles had declared himself against Quietism. But his noble and ingenuous soul was incapable of such a motive. The sweetness of his disposition and the idea that he had formed to himself of the goodness of God made him averse to the doctrine of Quesnel, which he considered as leading to despair. He consulted his own heart for arguments against it. "God," said he, "is to them only a terrible being; to one He is a being good and just. I cannot consent to make Him a tyrant who binds us with fetters and then commands us to walk and punishes us if we do not." But in proscribing principles that seemed to him too harsh and the consequences of which were disavowed by those who held them, he would not permit them to be persecuted. "Let us be to them," said he, "what they are unwilling that God should be to man, full of compassion and indulgence." He was told that the Jansenists were his declared enemies and that they left nothing undone to bring him and his doctrine into discredit. "That is one further reason," said he, "for me to suffer and forgive them."

Thus passed Fénelon's life till the melancholy death of the Duke of Burgundy in 1712. His death was a sad blight upon the fairest hopes of the nation. Fénelon's highest wishes seemed to be realized in him; the eyes and hopes of all were upon him. His veneration and his love for his preceptor had continued, and when he was allowed, he did not fail to express it. When Fénelon heard the afflicting intelligence of his death, he exclaimed, "All my ties are broken; nothing now remains to bind me to the earth." Shortly after, the Duke de Cheveruse, his intimate friend, died, and this was also a great sorrow to him. He wrote thus to a friend when he was deeply oppressed by these calamities: "Real friends are our greatest joy and our greatest sorrow. It were almost to be wished that all true and faithful friends should expire on the same day." All his letters written during this period show how deeply he suffered.

Fénelon had one more severe trial to endure. The Duke de Beauvilliers, to whom he was tenderly attached, and who, being governor to the Duke of Burgundy, was not permitted to see him after his banishment, died in 1714. Fénelon survived him but four months. The death of the Duke de Beauvilliers was the severe blow that finally subdued the tender heart of Fénelon. His frame was feeble; a severe shock that he received from the upsetting of his carriage induced a fever, and he died on the first of January 1715. In the last letter he wrote with his own hand, which was to the Duchess of Beauvilliers, he said to her, "We will soon find again that which we have not lost. We daily approach it with rapid strides. Yet a little while, and there will be no more cause for tears." He was taken sick and died three days after, at the age of sixty-five. In his last sickness, he displayed the most admirable fortitude and submission. There was the same sweetness of temper, composure of mind, love for his fellow creatures, and confidence in God that became the Christian and the friend of God and man that had distinguished his whole life.

The death of Fénelon was deeply lamented by all the inhabitants of the Low Countries. So extensive had been his charities, and yet so well-balanced his worldly affairs, that he died without money and without a debt. The following portrait of this celebrated prelate was given by the Duke de Saint Simon in his memoirs.

He was a tall, lean, well-made man with a large nose, eyes full of fire and intelligence, a physiognomy resembling none which I have elsewhere seen, and which could not be forgotten after it had been once beheld. There was such a sublime simplicity in his appearance that it required an effort to cease to look at him. His manners corresponded to his face and person. They were marked with that ease that makes others easy; there was an inexpressible air of good taste and refinement in them. He possessed a natural eloquence; a ready, clear, and agreeable elocution; and a power of making himself understood upon the most perplexed and abstract subjects. With all this, he never wished to appear wiser or wittier than those with whom he conversed but descended to everyone's level with a manner so free and so captivating that it was scarcely possible to leave him.

When we speak of the death of Fénelon, we realize the truth of what we all acknowledge, though few feel—that the good man never dies; that, to use the words of one of our eloquent divines, "death was but a circumstance in his being." We may say, as we read his writings, that we are conscious of his immortality. He is with us, his spirit around us. It enters into and takes possession of our souls. He is at this time, as he was when living in his diocese, the familiar friend of the poor and the sorrowful, the bold reprover of vice, and the gentle guide of the wanderer. He still says to all, in the words of his Divine Master, "Come to me, all ye that are heavy laden, and I will give you rest." (See Matthew 11:28.)

In the houses of the unlearned, where the names of Louis XIV and Bossuet have never entered, except as connected with Fénelon's, where not a word of his native tongue would be understood, his spirit has entered as a minister of love and wisdom, and a well-worn translation of his *Reflections*, with a short memoir of his life, is laid upon the precious Word of God. What has thus immortalized Fénelon? For what is he thus cherished in our hearts? Is it his learning? His celebrity? His eloquence? No, it is the spirit of Christian love, the spirit of the Savior of mankind, that is poured forth from all his writings—of that love that conquers self, that binds us to our neighbor, and that raises us to God. This is Fénelon's power; it is this that touches our souls. We feel that he has entered into the full meaning of that sublime passage in 1 John and made it the motto of his life: *"Beloved, let us love one another: for love is of God; and every one that loveth is born of God, and knoweth God. He that loveth not knoweth not God; for God is love"* (1 John 4:7–8).

II

SELECTIONS
FROM FÉNELON

ON THE
EXISTENCE OF GOD

Drawn from a View of Nature
and the Mind of Man

I cannot open my eyes without admiring the skill that everything in nature displays. A single glance enables me to perceive the hand that has made all things. Men who are accustomed to meditating upon abstract truths and returning to first principles recognize the Divinity by the idea of Him they find in their minds. But the more direct this road is, the more untrodden and neglected is it by common men, who follow their own imagination. It is so simple a demonstration that, from this very cause, it escapes those minds that are incapable of a purely intellectual operation. And the more perfect this way of discovering the Supreme Being is, the fewer are the minds that can follow it.

But there is another less perfect method that is adapted to the capacity of all. Those who exercise their reason the least, those who are the most affected by their senses, may at a single glance discover Him who is represented in all His works. The wisdom and power that God has manifested in everything that He has made reflects the name, as in a mirror, of Him whom they have not been able to discover in their own minds. This is a popular philosophy, addressed to the senses, that everyone without prejudice or passion is capable of acquiring.

A man whose whole heart is engaged in some grand concern might pass many days in a room attending to his affairs without seeing either the proportions of the room, the ornaments on the chimney, or the pictures that surrounded him. All these objects would be before his eyes, but he would not see them, and they would make no impression upon him. Thus it is that men live. Everything presents God to them, but they do not see Him. He was in the world, and the world was made by Him; nevertheless, the world has not known Him. They pass their lives without perceiving this representation of the Deity because the fascinations of life so completely obscure their vision.

Saint Augustine says that the wonders of the universe are lowered in our estimation by their repetition. Cicero says the same thing: "Forced to witness the same things every day, the mind as well as the eye is accustomed to them. It does not admire, or take any pains to discover, the cause of events that it always observes to take place in just the same way, as if it were the novelty rather than the grandeur of a thing that should lead us to this investigation."

But all nature shows the infinite skill of its Author. I maintain that accident—that is to say, a blind and fortuitous succession of events—could never have produced all that we see. It is well to adduce here one of the celebrated comparisons of the ancients.

Who would believe that the *Iliad* of Homer was not composed by the effort of a great poet but that the characters of the alphabet were thrown confusedly together and, by an accidental stroke, placed precisely in such relative situations as to produce verses so full of harmony and variety, painting each object with all that was most noble, most graceful, and most touching in its features and making each person speak in character and with such spirit and nature? Let anyone reason with as much subtileness as he may; he would persuade no man in his senses that the *Iliad* had no author but accident. Why then should a man, possessing his reason, believe with regard to the universe—a work unquestionably more wonderful than the *Iliad*—something that his good sense will not allow him to believe of this poem?

But let us take another comparison, which is from Gregory Nazianzen. If we heard, in a room behind a curtain, a sweet and harmonious instrument, could we believe that accident produced it? Who would doubt seriously whether some skilful hand did not touch it?

Were anyone to find, on a desert island, a beautiful statue of marble, he would say, "Surely men have been here. I recognize the hand of the sculptor; I admire the delicacy with which he has proportioned the body, making it instinct with beauty, grace, majesty, tenderness, and life."

Consider this man's reply if anyone said to him, "No, a sculptor did not make this statue. It is made, it is true, in the most exquisite taste and according to the most perfect rules of symmetry, but it is accident that has produced it. Among all the pieces of marble, one has happened to take this form of itself. The rains and the wind detached it from the mountain; a violent storm placed it upright upon this pedestal, which was already prepared, and placed here of itself. It is an Apollo as perfect as that of Belvedere; it is a Venus equal to that of the Medicis; it is a Hercules that resembles that of Farnese. You may believe, it is true, that this figure walks, that it lives, that it thinks, that it is going to speak. But it owes nothing to art; it is only a blind stroke of chance that has formed it so well and placed it here."

What should we say to a man who would pride himself upon superior knowledge and philosophy, and who, entering a house, would maintain that it was made by chance and that art and industry had done nothing to render it a commodious habitation for men, and who would give, as a reason, that there were caverns that resembled it that the art of man had not made?

We should show to him who reasoned in this way all the different parts of the house and their uses. It must be, we should say to this philosopher, that this work has been conducted by some able architect, for all parts of it are agreeable, pleasing to the eye, well proportioned, convenient. He must also have employed excellent workmen. "Not at all," this philosopher would say; "you are ingenious in self-deception. It is true that the house is pleasant, well proportioned, and commodious; but it is self-formed, with all its ingenious contrivances. Chance has collected and arranged these stones in this beautiful order. It has raised these walls, pierced these windows, placed the staircases. Do not believe that the hand of man had anything to do with it. Men have only occupied it when they found it finished. They imagine that it is made for them, because they find in it things that they can turn to their accommodation; but all that they attribute to the design of an architect is only the effect of their inventions afterward. This house, so regular and so well arranged, was made just as caverns are made; and finding it convenient, men have occupied it just as they would a cave that they should happen to find under a rock during a storm in the midst of a desert."

What would you think of this whimsical philosopher if he were to persist in arguing seriously that this house was not the product of any art? When we read the fable of Amphion, who by a miraculous harmony raised the stones one upon another, in order and symmetry, to form the walls of Thebes, we smile at the fiction of the poet; but this fiction is not as incredible as that which this philosopher maintains.

But why do we smile less at hearing that the world is a work of chance than we do that this fabulous house is? We do not compare the world to the cavern that we suppose was made by accident, but we may to a house in which is displayed the most perfect architecture. The smallest animal has a construction that is more admirable than that of the most perfect house.

A traveler entering Saide, which is the place, now a desert, that was once ancient Thebes, with its hundred gates, would find there columns, pyramids, obelisks, and inscriptions in unknown characters. Would he say, "Men have never inhabited this place; the hand of man has never been employed here; it is chance that has formed these columns and placed them upon their pedestals and crowned them with capitals in such beautiful proportions; it is chance that has hewn these obelisks out of single stones and that has engraved upon them all these hieroglyphics"? Would he not, on the contrary, say, with all the certainty of which the mind of man is capable, that these magnificent ruins are the remains of a majestic architecture that flourished in ancient Egypt?

This is what our reason would pronounce at the first glance. It is the same thing when we first contemplate the universe. People perplex themselves with sophistry and obscure their view of the simplest truths. But a glance is sufficient; such a work as this world could not have been made by chance.

The bones, the tendons, the veins, the arteries, the nerves, and the muscles that compose the body of a single man display more art and proportion than all the architecture of the ancient Greeks and Egyptians. The eye of the meanest animal surpasses the skill of all the artisans in the world.

But let us, before we proceed to the details of nature, fix our attention for a while upon the general structure of the universe. Cast your eyes upon the earth that supports us; raise them then to this immense vault of the heavens that surrounds us, these fathomless abysses of air and water, and these countless stars that give us light. Who has suspended this globe of earth? Who has laid its foundations? If it was harder, its bosom could not be laid open by man for cultivation; if it was less firm, it could not support the weight of his footsteps. From it proceed the most precious things. This earth, so mean and unformed, is transformed into thousands of beautiful objects that delight our eyes; in the course of one year, it becomes branches, buds, leaves, flowers, fruits, and seeds, thus renewing its bountiful favors to man. Nothing exhausts it. After yielding its treasures, it experiences no decay; it does not grow old. It still pours forth riches from its bosom. Generations of men have grown old and passed away, while every spring, the earth has renewed its youth. If it was cultivated, it would nourish a hundred-fold more than it now does.

The inequalities of the earth add to its beauty and utility. *"They go up by the mountains; they go down by the valleys unto the place which thou hast founded for them"* (Psalm 104:8). In the deep valleys grows the fresh herbage for cattle. Rich harvests wave in the champaign[2] country. Here ranges of little hills rise like an amphitheatre and are crowned with vineyards and fruit trees; there high mountains lift their snow-crowned heads among the clouds. The torrents that pour from their sides are the sources of the rivers. The rocks, marking their steep heights, support the earth of the mountains just as the bones of the human body support the flesh. This variety makes the charm of rural scenery, while it is also the means of satisfying all the different wants of men.

Everything that the earth produces is decomposed and returns again to its bosom and becomes the germ of a new production. Everything that springs from it returns to it, and nothing is lost. All the seeds that we sow in it return multiplied to us. It produces stone and marble, of which we make our superb edifices. It teems with minerals, precious or useful to man. Look at the plants that spring from it. Their species and their virtues are innumerable. Contemplate these vast forests, as ancient as the world—those trees whose roots strike into the earth as their branches spread out toward the heavens. Their roots support them against the winds and are like subterranean pipes, whose office is to collect the nourishment

---

2. *champaign*: level topography, as in a plain

necessary for the support of the stem. The stem is covered with a thick bark, which protects the tender wood from the air, and the branches distribute, in different canals, the sap that the roots have collected in the trunk. In summer, they protect us with their shade from the rays of the sun; in winter, they feed the flame that keeps as warm. Their wood is not only useful for fuel, but it is of a substance, although solid and durable, to which the hand of man can give every form that he pleases for the purposes of architecture and navigation. Fruit trees, as they bow their branches toward the earth, seem to invite us to receive their treasures. The feeblest plant contains within itself the germ of all that we admire in the grandest tree. The earth that does not change itself produces all these changes in its offspring.

Let us notice what we call water; it is a liquid, clear, and transparent body. Now it escapes from our grasp, and now it takes the form of whatever surrounds it, having none of its own. If the water were a little more rarefied, it would become a species of air; the whole face of nature would be dry and sterile. He who has given us this fluid body has distributed it with care through the earth. The waters flow from the mountains. They assemble in streams in the valleys, and they flow on in rivers, winding their way through the open country so that they may more effectually water it. At last they empty themselves into the sea to feed this center of the commerce of nations. This ocean that seems an eternal separation of countries is, on the contrary, the great rendezvous of all nations. It is over this pathless way, across this profound abyss, that the old world has put forth its hand to the new, and that the new supplies the old with its treasures.

The waters circulate through the earth as the blood does through the human body. Besides this perpetual circulation, there is the ebbing and flowing of the sea. We need not know the cause of this mysterious effect. This we are certain of only, that the sea goes and returns to the same places at certain hours. Who has commanded it to ebb and flow with such regularity? A little more or a little less motion in the waters would derange all nature. Who is it that controls this immense body with such irresistible power? Who is it that always avoids the too much and the too little? What unerring finger has marked the boundaries for the sea that, through countless ages, it has respected, and has said to it, "Here shall your proud waves be stayed"?

If I look up to the heavens, I perceive clouds flying as upon the wings of the wind—bodies of water suspended over our heads to temper the air and water the thirsty earth. If they were to fall all at once, they would overwhelm and destroy everything in the place where they fell. What hand suspends them in their reservoirs and bids them fall drop by drop, as from a watering pot?

We have considered the waters; let us notice other bodies of still greater extent. The air is so subtile, so transparent, that the stars at an almost infinite distance pierce through it with their light. We live immersed in the abysses of air, as fish do in the depths of the waters. As the waters, if they were rarefied, would become a species of air that would destroy them, so too the air would destroy us if it were more dense and humid. Who is it that has composed the air so exactly for our respiration? What power unseen excites and stills so suddenly the tempests of this vast fluid body? From what storehouse are the winds drawn that purify the air, that temper the seasons, and that change the face of the heavens in an instant, wafting the clouds on the wings of the wind from one edge of the horizon to the other?

Let us fix our attention upon the flame that lights up the stars and spreads its light over the universe. The mountains vomit the fire that the earth has held in its bosom. This same fire remains unseen in the veins of the flint and waits for the blow that will excite it and make it kindle mountains. Mankind has learned the way to obtain it and subject it to their use, to make it bend the hardest metals, to feed and cherish it in cold climates, and to make it take the place of the absent sun. Fire penetrates all seeds. It is as the soul of everything that lives; it consumes all that is impure and renews what it has first purified. The ancients worshipped fire; they believed that it was a celestial treasure that mankind had stolen from the gods.

But it is time to raise our eyes to the heavens. Who has stretched over our heads this vast and glorious vault? What sublime objects are there! An all-powerful hand has presented this grand spectacle to our vision. It is, says Cicero, in order that we may admire the heavens that God has formed man differently from other animals. He is made upright and lifts his head that he may contemplate that which is above him.

What does the regular succession of day and night teach us? The sun has never failed, for so many ages, to shed his blessing upon us. Aurora never fails to announce the day; she appears at the appointed time and in the fixed place, and the sun, says the Holy Book, knows it's going down. Thus it enlightens alternately both sides of the world, and sheds its rays on all. Day is the time for society and employment. Night folds the world in darkness, finishes our labors, and softens our troubles. It suspends, it calms, everything. It sheds round us silence and sleep; it rests our bodies and revives our spirits. Then day returns and reanimates all nature, calling man back to labor.

Besides the constant course of the sun that produces day and night, during six months it approaches one pole and, during the other six, the opposite one. By this beautiful order, one sun answers for the whole world. If the sun at the same distance were larger, it would light the whole world, but it would consume it with its heat. If it were smaller, the earth would be all ice and could not be inhabited by men. What compass has been stretched from heaven to earth and taken such just measurements? The changes of the sun make the variety of the seasons, which we find so delightful. The spring checks the cold winds, wakens the flowers, and gives the promise of fruits. The summer brings the riches of the harvest. The autumn displays the fruits that spring has promised. Winter, which is the night of the year, treasures up all its riches, only in order that the following spring may bring them forth again with new beauty.

Thus nature, so variously adorned, presents alternately her beautiful changes, that man may never cease to admire.

Let us look up again at this immense concave above us, where sparkle the countless stars. If it is solid, who is the architect? Who has fastened in it at regular distances such grand and luminous bodies? Who makes this vaulted sky turn around us so regularly? If, on the contrary, the heavens are only immense spaces filled with fluid bodies, like the air that surrounds us, how is it that so many solid bodies float in it without interfering one with another? After so many ages, as men have been making astronomical observations, they have discovered no derangement in the heavens. Can a fluid body give such a constant and regular order to the substances that float on its bosom? But what is this almost countless multitude of stars for? God has sown them in the heavens as a magnificent prince would adorn his garments with precious stones.

But someone may say, "These are all worlds like the earth we inhabit." Suppose it be so. How wise and powerful must He be who has made worlds as innumerable as the grains of sand on the seashore and who has led on in order for so many ages all these moving worlds as a shepherd leads his flocks? The motion of the stars, it is said, is regulated by immutable laws. This very fact will prove what I wish to establish. Who is it that has given laws to all nature so constant and so salutary? Laws so simple that people are tempted to believe they established themselves, so full of utility that we cannot help recognizing in them a miraculous skill? From whence comes the power that conducts this admirable machine of the universe that is ever moving for us without our thinking of it? To whom will we attribute this assemblage of so many means that are so wonderful and so well arranged—of so many bodies, great and small, visible and invisible? If the least atom of this machine were to become deranged, it would disorganize the universe. What is this design, so unlimited, so admirably pursued, so beautiful, so beneficent? The necessity of these laws, far from preventing me from seeking the Author, only increases my curiosity and my admiration. The hand that guides this glorious work must be as skillful as it is powerful, to have made it so simple yet so effectual, so constant and so beneficent. I am ready to exclaim, in the language of Scripture, "Every star makes haste to go where God commands it." (See Psalm 33:6–9.) When He speaks, they answer with trembling, "We are here."

But let us turn our attention to the animals, still more worthy of our admiration than the heavens and the stars. Their species are innumerable. The wings of birds and the fins of fishes are like oars, with which they cleave the waves of air or water and conduct the floating body of the bird or fish that is formed like a boat. The wings of birds have feathers that are covered with a soft down that expands in the air and would grow heavy in the water, but the fins of the fishes are of dry and hard, pointed bones that cut the water without imbibing it and do not become heavier from being wet. Some birds that swim, as the swan, lift up their wings and all their plumage, for fear of wetting it, and make use of it as sails. They have the art of turning it toward the wind and tacking like a vessel when it is not favorable.

Among animals, ferocious beasts, such as lions, have the largest muscles in the shoulders, thighs, and legs. These animals are also very supple, nervous, agile, and quick to spring. Their jaw bones are immense compared to the rest of the body. They have teeth and tusks that serve them as terrible weapons against their prey. Some animals, like the tortoise, carry about with them the house in which they were born; others build theirs, like the birds, upon the high branches of trees, to preserve their little ones from being injured by animals without wings. They place their nests amid the thickest foliage to hide them from their enemies. The beaver builds for himself an asylum at the very bottom of the water and raises dikes to secure it from inundation. The fox makes his burrow with two openings, so that he may, if surprised, escape the snares of the hunter. Birds, says Cicero, that have very long legs have also long necks, in proportion, so that they can reach the bottom and take their food. The elephant, whose neck would be too heavy if it was as long as the camel's, is provided with a long trunk, which is a succession of nerves and muscles, that it can stretch out and contract, that it can fold up and turn in any way it pleases, to seize anything or lift or repulse any object. The Romans called it a hand.

Certain animals seem made for man. The dog seems born for his caresses and his service. The horse seems born to carry his burdens, to support him in his weakness, and to obey his will. The ox has the strength and patience that are wanted to drag the plough. The cow refreshes him with her milk. The sheep has a superfluous clothing that is continually renewed, as if to invite man to accept it. Even goats have a sort of long hair that is useless to them and of which men make clothing. The skins of animals, in cold countries, supply the inhabitants with the most beautiful furs. Thus the Author of nature has clothed the brute creation according to their necessities, and their apparel serves for the use of man.

If any animal appears useless to us, we ought to consider that whatever makes a part of this grand spectacle of nature is not without its use in the eyes of those who think and attend to it. What is there more magnificent than those various republics of animals, all so well governed and different from each other? Everything demonstrates to us how far the skill of the workman surpasses the vile material that he employs. Everything astonishes me, even the structure of the smallest fly. We find in the most insignificant worm, as in an elephant or in a whale, perfectly organized members. We see in it a head and body—limbs as in the greatest animals. There are, in each part of these living atoms, muscles, nerves, veins, arteries, blood; in this blood, component parts and humors; in these humors, particles containing in themselves different substances; and we know not where to stop in the infinite process. The microscope uncovers to us in every object a thousand things that have escaped our observation. Within these, how many wonders are there that the microscope cannot uncover to us? What might we see if we could continually improve the instruments that we use in aid of our feeble vision? But let our imagination be a sort of microscope by which we may see, in every atom, thousands of new and invisible worlds; it could only present to us new discoveries in the smallest bodies. We should be wearied, and, at last, we should leave, in the smallest organ, a thousand unknown wonders.

Let us dwell for a while upon the animal machine. Animals have what we call instinct, which enables them to pursue what is useful and avoid what is hurtful. We need not seek to know what this instinct is; let us be contented with the simple fact without reasoning about it. The lamb knows its mother at a distance. The sheep is conscious of the approach of the wolf before she can see him. There is in all animals a contingent power that enables them to collect their faculties in an instant, that braces their nerves, that renders their joints supple, and that gives them, in sudden danger, an almost miraculous agility, strength, and adroitness in escaping from their enemy. It is instinct, it is said, that guides animals. I grant it. It is in truth an instinct, but this instinct is a most admirable sagacity and dexterity, not in the animals, who have not the power at the time to reason, but in that superior wisdom that directs them.

This instinct, or this wisdom, that thinks and watches over animals in unexpected circumstances when they could not reason or protect themselves, even if they had our reason, can only be the wisdom of the workman who has made the machine. Let us then no longer speak of instinct or nature; these are only empty sounds in the mouths of those who repeat them. There is, in what we call nature and instinct, an art, an admirable skill, of which human invention is only the image. This is indubitable; there are in animals an immense number of movements entirely unpremeditated that are performed according to the most perfect rules of mechanics. It is the machine obeying its laws. This is the fact, independent of all philosophy, and the fact is enough. What should we think of a watch that was able to defend itself or escape when anyone desired to break it? Should we not admire the skill of the workman? Could we believe that this watch could be formed, proportioned, and arranged by mere chance? Would we think that these operations were satisfactorily explained by saying, "It is nature or instinct that makes this watch tell its master the hours and escape from those who wish to hurt it"?

What can be more perfect than a machine that ever renews and repairs itself? As the animal is limited in its strength, it is soon exhausted by labor; but the more it is used, the more it is prompted to compensate for its losses by an abundant nourishment. Food restores the waste of every day. A foreign substance enters the body and, by a strange metamorphosis, becomes a part of it. First it is ground up and changed into a liquid; then it is purified, as if it were passed through a sieve in order to separate the parts of it that are too gross. Then it passes to the center, where it goes through a process by which it is refined and turned into blood; and at last it flows through innumerable channels and waters to all the members of the body and insinuates itself through the whole frame; it is filtrated by the flesh as it passes, finally becoming flesh itself. So many different solids and liquids become all the same substance. The food that was only an inanimate body becomes a living animal. What was not long since a horse is now only a vapor or air. What was only hay or oats has become that noble, high-spirited animal. He passes for the same animal, notwithstanding this insensible change in his substance.

To nourishment is added sleep. All external motions cease, and even all the interior operations that might agitate and dissipate the spirits; nothing remains but digestion and respiration. That is to say, everything is suspended that requires effort, and everything necessary for renovation is active and free. This repose, which seems a sort of enchantment, returns every night while the darkness interrupts labor. Who has contrived this suspension? Who is it that has so well chosen the operations of this machine that ought to proceed, and stopped so wisely those that should be at rest? The next morning, all its fatigues have passed away. The animal labors as if he had never labored before, and in consequence of the renovation, there is a vivacity and spirit in him that invites to new exertion.

Let us stop no longer at the inferior animals. It is time to study the structure of the human frame of man, so that we may discover Him in whose image he is made. I see in all nature but two kinds of beings—those who have knowledge and those who have none. Man unites in his nature these two forms of being. He has a body like the most inanimate beings, and he has a soul—a power of thought by which he knows himself and perceives all that is around him. If it is true that there is a Being who has drawn everything from nothing, man is His true image, for he unites in his nature the perfection of those two forms of being. But the image is only an image; it can only be a shadow of the truly perfect Being.

Let us begin with the body of man; it is made from clay, but let us admire the hand that has fashioned it. The stamp of the workman is imprinted on His work; it seems to have been His pleasure to make of such worthless materials a perfect work. Observe the bones that support the flesh, which surrounds them; the nerves, which give it strength; the muscles, which, by being expanded or lengthened, produce the most certain and regular motions. The bones are separated at certain distances and are fitted one to another and fastened by nerves and tendons. Cicero admired, with good reason, the beautiful contrivance that unites the bones. What can be more supple and adapted to different motions, but what is there more firm and durable? Thus this machine is erect or bent, stiff or flexible, as we wish it.

From the brain, which is the source of all the nerves, flows the vital principle. It is too subtle to be discerned but nevertheless is real and so active that it produces all the motions and all the strength of the machine. It flies in an instant to the farthest extremity of the body. Now it moves gently and with uniformity, now with a violent impetuosity; it varies unceasingly with the different situations of the body.

The flesh is covered in certain parts with a thin and delicate skin for the ornament of the body. In some parts, this skin is harder and thicker than in others so that it may resist the wear upon it. For instance, how much thicker the skin on the sole of the foot than the face; on the back part than on the front of the head. This skin is pierced everywhere like a sieve with small holes; these are called pores. While the perspiration is insensibly exhaled through them, the blood never escapes. The skin has all the delicacy necessary to make it transparent and to give to the countenance an animated and beautiful color. Who has tempered and mingled these colors so as to produce this brilliant carnation that painters admire and vainly endeavor to imitate?

We find in the human body innumerable channels. Some carry the blood from the center to the extremities and are called arteries; others return it from the extremities to the center and are called veins. Through all these various canals, the blood flows; it is a soft, unctuous liquid that is calculated from this quality to preserve the most delicate substances, as we preserve essences in gums. This blood waters the flesh as rivers water the earth. After being filtered by what it has passed through, it returns to its source slowly, having been divested of the vital principle. But it renews and refreshes itself again, and so circulates perpetually.

Who can explain the delicacy of the organs by which we discover the taste of such a variety of bodies? How is it that so many voices strike my ear at the same time and produce no confusion, and that, after they are gone, these sounds leave with me such lively and distinct resemblances of what they were? With what care has He who made our bodies provided our eyes with a moist and moving envelope to close them with. And why has He left our ears always open? Who is it that paints on my eye, in an instant, the heavens, the ocean, the earth? How is it that on such a little organ, faithful images of every object in nature, from the sun to the motes in his beams, are depicted and clearly defined?

This substance of the brain that preserves in order these lively representations of the glorious objects that we see in the universe is a most wonderful thing. We admire with reason the invention of books, in which are preserved the histories of so many facts, and which are the depositaries of so many thoughts.

But what comparison is there between the most delightful book and the brain of a learned man? There can be no doubt that this brain is a far more precious collection and a much more beautiful invention than any book. In this little reservoir, you can find at any moment every image that you desire. You call them, and they come. You send them away, and they hide themselves—we know not where—and others appear in their place. We open and shut our imaginations as we open and shut a book; as one may say, we turn over its leaves and pass suddenly from one end of it to the other. We have even tablets in the memory to indicate the places where certain images may be found. These innumerable characters, which the mind can read so rapidly, leave no traces on the brain. If you examine it, you see only a soft substance, a sort of cluster of fine, tender, and twisted threads. What hand has hidden in this apparently shapeless matter such precious images and arranged them there in such beautiful order?

But the body of man, which seems the *chef-d'oeuvre* of nature, is not comparable to his soul. How is it that beings so unlike are united in man's composition? How is it that the movements of the body give so infallibly and so promptly certain thoughts to the soul? How is it that the thoughts of the soul produce certain movements of the body? How is it that this harmonious connection exists without interruption for seventy or eighty years? How is it that two beings, possessing such different operations, make a whole so perfect that some are tempted to believe that they are one and indivisible?

What hand has united these two extremes? Matter could not make an agreement with spirit. The spirit has no recollection of making any compact with matter. Nevertheless, it is certain that it is dependent on the body and that it cannot be freed from its power unless it destroys it by a violent death. This dependence is reciprocal. Nothing is more absolute than the empire of the soul over the body. The spirit wills, and every member of the body is instantly moved, as if it were impelled by some powerful machine. What hand, holding an equal power over both these natures, has imposed this yoke upon them and held them captive in a connection so nice and so inviolable? Can anyone say, "Chance"? They do, but can they understand what they say themselves and make others comprehend it? Has chance linked together the particles of body with soul by a concourse of atoms?

My alternative is this: If the soul and the body are only a composition of matter, why is it that this matter, which did not think yesterday, begins to think today? Who is it that has given it what it did not before possess, and what is incomparably more noble than itself, when it was without thought? Does not that which bestows thought possess it? Suppose even that thought resulted from a certain configuration and arrangement and motion of matter; what workman has discovered these just and nice combinations so as to make a thinking machine? If, on the contrary, the soul and the body are two distinct substances, what power superior to both these different natures has bound them together? Who, with a supreme empire over both, has sent forth his command that they should be linked together by a correspondence and in a civil subjection that is incomprehensible?

The empire of my mind over my body is despotic to a certain extent, since my simple will, without effort or preparation, can move every member of my body by mechanical rules. As the Scriptures represent God, in the creation, to have said, *"Let there be light: and there was light"* (Genesis 1:3), so the voice of my soul speaks, and my body obeys. This is the power that men who believe in God attribute to Him over the universe.

This power of the soul over the body, which is so absolute, is at the same time a blind one. The most ignorant man moves his body as well as the best instructed anatomist. The player on the lute, who perfectly understands all the chords of his instrument, who sees it with his eyes and touches it with his fingers, often makes mistakes. But the soul that governs the machine of the human body can move every spring without seeing it, without seeing or understanding its figure, or situation, or strength, and never makes mistakes. How wonderful is this! My soul commands what it does not know, what it cannot see, and what it is itself incapable of knowing, and it is infallibly obeyed. How great its ignorance, and how great its power! The blindness is ours, but the power—where is it from? To whom can we attribute it, if not to the One who sees what man cannot see and who gives him the power to perform what surpasses his own comprehension?

The truth is, we cannot admire too much this absolute empire of the soul over the organs it does not understand and the continual use it makes of them. This is principally shown in recalling images traced on the brain. I am acquainted with all the objects of the universe that have impressed my senses for a great number of years; I have distinct images of them, so that I can think I see them when they are no more. My brain is a cabinet of pictures, every one of which is brought forward or removed according to the taste of the master of the mansion. By the portraits that I have in my head, I judge whether the artist's picture is a faithful representation. It is by consulting them that I ascertain where his defects are. Such wonders astonish me. I remember distinctly having known that which I no longer know. I recall the face of every person in every age of life in which I have known him. The same person passes in different forms through my mind. First I see him a child, then a man, and at last old. I place the wrinkles upon the same face in which I have seen the tender and lovely traits of childhood. I join that which is no more with what now exists, without confounding their outlines. I preserve in this storehouse a something that has been successively everything I have known since I was born. From this treasure spring all the perfumes, all the harmony, all the tastes, all the degrees of light, all the bright colors, and all their shades—in short, all the forms that have been presented to my senses and that they have conveyed to my brain.

I recall, when I please, the joy that I experienced thirty years ago. It returns, but it is not the same. It appears, but it does not rejoice me. I remember that I was glad, but I am not so at the remembrance. On the other hand, I bring back departed sorrows.

They are present with me, for I perceive them just as they were at the time. Nothing escapes me of their bitterness and of the acuteness of the feeling. But they are not the same thing. They trouble me no longer; they are softened. I see all their severity without feeling it, or if I feel it, it is only as a representation. It is like a scene of a play. The images of past griefs give us pleasure. It is the same with our pleasures. A virtuous heart is afflicted at the recollection of its unworthy pleasures. They are present to us, but they are no longer themselves; such joys return only to bid us weep. Chance surely never created this wonderful book; all the art of man is unequal to such perfection. What hand has made it?

Let us conclude these remarks by some reflections upon the nature of the mind of man. I find in it an incomprehensible mixture of greatness and weakness. Its grandeur is real. It connects, without confusion, the past with the present, and it penetrates into the future; it has an idea of matter and of spirit. It has within it the idea even of infinity, for it will deny all that does not belong to it and affirm all that does.

Say that infinity is triangular, and it will instantly answer that something that has no limits cannot have any form. Ask it to name the first unit of an infinite number, and it will readily answer that there can be neither beginning, nor end, nor number in infinity. It is through the infinite that it comes to the knowledge of the finite.

How glorious is the spirit that is in man; it bears itself what is far beyond its own comprehension. Its ideas are universal, eternal, and immutable. They are universal, because, when I say, "It is impossible to be and not to be"; "The whole is greater than a part"; "A perfectly circular line has no straight parts"; "Between two given points, the straightest line is the shortest"; "The center of a circle is equally distant from all the points in its circumference"—none of these truths can be controverted. There can be no line or circle that does not obey these laws. These truths are of all time or, rather, before all time, and they will continue beyond it through an incomprehensible duration.

Let the universe be overthrown and annihilated, let there be no minds to reason upon these truths; they will still remain equally true, as the rays of the sun would be no less real if men were blind and could not see them. In feeling assured, says Saint Augustine, that two and two make four, we are not only certain that we say what is true, but we have no doubt that this proposition has been always, and will continue to be, eternally true.

These fundamental ideas have no limits and cannot be changed. What I have advanced of one circle, we acknowledge to be necessarily true of all circles to infinity. These ideas that are illimitable can never change or be effaced or impaired; they are the foundations of our reason. It is impossible, whatever power we may exert over our minds, to make ourselves seriously doubt anything that these ideas represent to us. The idea of infinity is within us in like manner. Change these ideas, and you overthrow reason. Let us learn the greatness of our natures from this immutable idea of infinity that is imprinted within us and that can never be effaced. But, lest our real greatness dazzle our eyes and flatter us to our injury, let us hasten to contemplate our weakness.

This same mind that dwells upon the infinite, and through it sees the finite, is ignorant of all that surrounds it. It does not know itself. It gropes its way through an abyss of darkness. It knows not what it is itself; it does not comprehend how it is chained to this body or how it has such an empire over it. It is ignorant of its own thoughts and its own desires; it does not know with certainty what it believes or what it desires. It often deceives itself, and its highest attainment is to understand itself. It joins errors in opinion to a perverted will, and it is often reduced to groan and weep at the experience of its own corruption.

Such is the spirit of man—weak, uncertain, limited, and full of imperfections. Who has given the idea of infinity (that is, perfection) to a being so shortsighted and full of imperfection? Has he given to himself this thought that is so high and pure, that is in itself an image of the infinite? Let us suppose that the spirit of man is like a mirror in which the images of all the surrounding objects are reflected; from whence does this image of the infinite come? How can the image of an unreal object be reflected there? The infinite is there represented, but not by a confused mass of finite objects that the mind mistakes for the infinite; it is the true infinite that is presented to our thoughts. We understand it well; we recognize it and distinguish it from all that it is not. No subtileness can put any other object in its place.

From whence does this glorious image come? Do we draw it out of nothing? Can the finite and limited being invent and imagine the infinite, if it does not exist? External objects cannot give us this image, for they can give us only the images of themselves, and they are all limited and imperfect. From whence do we draw this distinct representation of the infinite, which is unlike all that we know and all that exists without us? From whence does it come? Where is this infinite that we cannot comprehend and yet cannot mistake? Where does it dwell? If it did not exist, could it be so engraved in the depths of our souls?

But besides this idea of infinity, I have general and immutable ideas that are the rule of all my judgments. I cannot decide upon anything without consulting them, and it is out of my power to decide against what they represent to me. My thoughts, far from being able to correct or form this rule, are themselves corrected, in spite of myself, by this superior power and are irresistibly subjected to its decisions.

I cannot, as I before said, doubt that two and two make four—and so of other mathematical truths. I am not free to deny them. This fixed and immutable law is so inwrought that it seems like my identity, but it is above me, since it corrects, rectifies, and guides me, teaching me my own weakness and imperfection. It is something that will ever inspire me, if I listen to it; and I always err when I do not attend to it.

This principle will guide me right if I am docile, for this inspiration of the Almighty will enable me to judge of the things that are around me and on which I am called to decide. And of all other things, it will teach me not to judge—a no less important lesson than the first. This interior guide is what I call my *reason*, but I speak of my reason without comprehending the full import of the term, just as I speak of *nature* and *instinct* without comprehending what these things are. This law is perfect and immutable. I am changing and imperfect. Thus, I deceive myself, while this law never loses its rectitude. When I am undeceived, it is not my reason that changes and returns to the right view, but it is this law, which has never departed from perfection, that recalls and forces me to return to it. It is a controlling power within me that silences or bids me speak, that makes me believe or makes me doubt, that bids me confess my errors or confirms my decisions. In listening to it, I am instructed; in listening to myself, I go astray. This sovereign power is found everywhere; its voice is heard from one end of the universe to the other by all mankind as it is by me.

Two men who have never seen each other, who have never heard each other spoken of, and who have had no communication with any other man that could give them common notions, would speak, at the two extremities of the world, of certain truths in perfect unison. We know perfectly well beforehand in one hemisphere what answer would be given on the other side of the world regarding certain truths. Men of all countries and of all times, whatever education they may have received, necessarily think and speak of some things in the same manner. It is the great Master who has taught us all and who thus bids us speak. Thus, when we think most of our own powers, of ourselves, and of our reason, it is this very part of our natures that least belongs to us and that is most truly a borrowed good.

We are, at every moment of our lives, receiving a reason far superior to ourselves, just as we inhale the air from without or see objects around us only by the light of the sun, which does not belong to our vision. It is this noble reason that reigns with an absolute dominion, to a certain point, over rational beings. It is this that makes a Canadian savage think many things that Greek and Roman philosophers have thought. It is this that led the Chinese geometricians to the discovery of the same truths that the Europeans, who knew nothing of them, have become acquainted with. It is this that makes men think upon various subjects just as they thought a thousand years ago. It is this power that gives uniformity to the opinions of men who are the most opposed to each other in their natures. It is by this that men of all ages and countries are bound to an immovable center by certain invariable laws, which we call first principles—notwithstanding the infinite variety of opinions that are created by their passions, distractions, and caprices upon all other less clear truths. It is this power that has kept men, depraved as they are, from daring to call virtue vice, and that has obliged them to put on the appearance, at least, of sincerity, moderation, and beneficence when they would attract esteem.

They cannot esteem or despise anything according to their own arbitrary wills; they cannot force the eternal barriers of truth and justice. The law of the soul, which we call reason, reigns with an absolute sway. Its reproaches are ever uttered and repeated at what is wrong, and it sets boundaries to the folly of the most audacious.

After vice has enjoyed so many ages of unrestrained sway, virtue is still called virtue, and it cannot be dispossessed of its name by its boldest and most brutal enemies. Thus vice, although triumphant in the world, is still forced to disguise itself under the mask of hypocrisy so that it may secure a regard that it does not hope for when it is known as it is. Thus it renders, in spite of itself, homage to virtue by adorning itself with her charms, so that it may receive the honors that are rendered to them. Men cavil, it is true, at the virtuous, and they are, in truth, always liable to censure, for they are still imperfect. But the most vicious men cannot succeed in effacing entirely the idea of virtue. No man has ever succeeded in persuading others or himself that it is more estimable to be deceitful than to be sincere or to be violent and malignant than to be gentle and to do good. This inward, universal teacher declares the same truths at all times and places. It is true that we often contradict it and speak with a louder voice, but then we deceive ourselves, and we go astray. We fear that we will discover that we are wrong, and we shut our ears, lest we should be humbled by its corrections. Where is this wisdom? Where is this oracle that ever speaks and against which the prejudices of mankind can never prevail? Where is this noble reason that we are bound to consult and that, of itself, inspires us with a desire to hear its voice? Where dwells this pure and gentle light that not only enlightens eyes that are open to receive it but also uncloses those eyes that were shut, cures those that were diseased, gives vision to the blind, and, in short, inspires a desire for the light it can bestow, making itself beloved even to those who fear it?

Every eye has it; it would see nothing without it. It is by its pure rays alone that it can see anything. As the visible sun enlightens all material bodies, so the sun of intelligence illuminates all minds.

There is a spiritual sun that enlightens the soul more fully than the material sun does the body. This sun of truth leaves no shadow, and it shines upon both hemispheres. It is as brilliant in the night as in the daytime; it is not without that it sheds its rays, but it dwells within each one of us. One man cannot hide its rays from another; whatever corner of the earth we may go to, there it is. We never need say to another, "Stand back, that I may see it; you hide its rays from me; you deprive me of the portion that is my due." This glorious sun never sets; no clouds intercept its rays but those formed by our passions. It is one bright day. It sheds light upon the savage in the darkest caverns. There are no eyes so weak that they cannot bear its light, and there is no man so blind and miserable that he does not walk by the feeble light from this source that he still retains in his conscience.

We believe the instructions of men just in proportion to the conformity we find between them and this inward teacher. After they have exhausted all their reasonings, we still return to this and listen to the decision it makes. If anyone tells me that a part is equal to the whole, I cannot help laughing. Such a one cannot persuade me; it is within myself, by consulting this inward teacher, that I must ascertain the truth of a proposition. Far from pronouncing judgment upon this teacher, we are in all cases judged by it. It is disinterested and superior to us. We may refuse to listen to it, and go astray from it; but if we do listen, we cannot contradict it. There seem to be two kinds of reason within me—one is self, the other superior to it. That which is self is very imperfect—prejudiced, rash, apt to wander, changing, obstinate, ignorant, and limited. It possesses nothing that is not borrowed. The other, while it is common to all men, is yet superior to them. It is perfect, eternal, immutable, and always ready to be communicated and to reclaim the erring; given freely to all, it is inexhaustible and indivisible. Where is this all-perfect reason that is so near me yet so different from me? Where is it? Where does this supreme reason dwell? Is it not God Himself?

I find still further traces of the Divinity within me. I have within me a clear idea of a perfect unity that is far superior to what I can discover in my own soul, which is often divided between two opinions, between two inclinations, between two opposite habits. This division that I find within me proves a composition of parts and something more than one. My soul has at least a succession of thoughts, one very different from another. My idea of unity is, if I may use the expression, infinitely more one. I have a conception of a Being who never changes His thought, who has all thoughts at the same instant, who has no succession of ideas. It is doubtless this idea of a perfect and supreme unity in my own mind that makes me desirous to find a unity in the soul and even in matter. This idea, ever present to my spirit, must have been born with me. It is the perfect model, of which I am ever seeking the imperfect copy. This idea of what is simply and indivisibly one can only be the idea of God. I then know God with such certainty that, by this knowledge, I seek in every outward thing, and in myself, some resemblance to His unity.

Another mystery that I bear within me and that renders me incomprehensible to myself is that, on the one hand, I am free, and on the other, dependent. I must be dependent. Independence is the supreme perfection. The Creator must be the cause of all the modifications of His creation. The being who is dependent for his nature must be so for all its operations. Thus, God is the real cause of all the combinations and movements of everything in the universe. It is He who has created all that is.

But I am free, and I cannot doubt it; I have an intimate and immovable conviction that I am free to will or not to will. There is within me a power of election, not only to will or not, but to decide between different objects. This is in itself a proof of the immateriality of my soul. What is material and corporeal cannot choose; it is, on the contrary, governed by fixed laws that are called physical; they are necessary, invincible, and contrary to what I call liberty. In saying, then, that I am free, I say that my will is fully in my power and that God leaves it to me to use it as I am disposed. I am not determined by a law, like other beings, but I will of myself. I conceive that if the Supreme Being inspires me with a will to do right, I have the power to reject the inspiration, however great it might be—to frustrate its effect and to refuse my consent. I conceive, also, that when I reject His inspiration to do right, I have actually the power *not* to reject it, just as I have the power to open or shut my eyes.

Outward things may solicit me by all that is most captivating; the most powerful and affecting arguments may be presented to influence me, and the Supreme Being may touch my heart with the most persuasive inspirations. But I still remain free to will or not to will. It is this exemption from all restraint and from all necessity, this empire over my own actions, that makes me inexcusable when I will what is evil, and praiseworthy when I will what is good.

This is the foundation of all merit or demerit; it is this that makes the justice of reward or punishment. Hence it is that we exhort, reprove, menace, or promise. This is the foundation of all government, of all instruction, and of all rules of conduct. Everything in human life brings us to this conclusion—that there is nothing over which we have such entire control as our own wills, and that we have this free will, this power of election, between two things equally in our reach. It is this truth that the shepherds sing among the mountains, that merchants and artisans take for granted in their negotiations, that the actor represents on the stage, that the magistrate recognizes in his decisions, and that the learned doctors teach in their schools. It is what no man of sense can seriously doubt. This truth, imprinted on our hearts, is acknowledged in the practice of those philosophers who attempt to overthrow it by their chimerical[3] speculations. The internal evidence of this truth is like that we have of those first principles that have no need of demonstration and by which we prove other truths less certain.

Let us view together these equally undoubted truths. I am dependent upon the Supreme Being even for my will; nevertheless, I am free. What is this dependent liberty? How can we comprehend a will that is free and that is yet given by the Supreme Being? I am free in my will, as God is in His. It is in this, principally, that I am in His image and resemble Him. This is a grandeur that belongs to the Infinite Being, a trait of His celestial nature. It is a divine power that I possess over my will, but I am only a faint image of His all-powerful will.

My liberty is only a shadow of that of the Supreme Being, from whom I exist and from whom I act. On the other hand, the power I have of willing evil is not so much true power as it is the weakness and frailty of my will. It is a power to destroy, to degrade myself, to lessen my own perfection and being. On the other hand, the power I have of willing what is right is not an independent power, as I do not possess it in myself. A borrowed power can only confer a dependent liberty. How then is such a being free? What a deep mystery! A man's liberty, of which I cannot doubt, proves his perfection; his dependence shows the nothingness from which he has been drawn. *"For as the heavens are higher than the earth,"* says God in the Scriptures, *"so are my ways higher than your ways, and my thoughts than your thoughts"* (Isaiah 55:9).

---

3. *chimerical*: existing only as the product of unchecked imagination: fantastically visionary or improbable

We have thus followed the traces of the Divinity through what are called the works of nature. We may observe, at the first glance, an all-powerful hand that is the first mover of everything in every part of the universe. The heavens, the earth, the stars, the plants, the animals, our bodies, our spirits—all discover an order, a nice arrangement, a skill, and a wisdom far superior to our own, which is the soul of the whole world and which conducts everything to its destined end with a gentle and insensible but all-powerful sway. We have seen, if we may so speak, the architecture of the universe, the just proportions of all its parts. And one look is enough to show us, in an insect yet more than in the sun, a wisdom and a power that shine forth in its meanest works.

These are views that would strike the most ignorant. What would be our impressions if we could enter the secrets of the material world, if we could dissect the internal parts of animals and observe their perfect mechanism! Everything, then, in the universe, bears the marks of the Divinity, and man more than all the rest. Everything shows design to us and a connection of second causes that are directed by a first cause. We have no ground to cavil at this great work; the defects that we discover in it are produced by the ill-regulated but free will of man.

It often happens that what appears like a defect to our limited vision, when viewed separately from the whole, gives a beauty to the general design. We do not possess that enlargement and simplicity of mind by which alone we can comprehend the perfection of the whole. Does it not often happen that we hastily condemn parts of the works of men because we have not sufficiently penetrated into the whole extent of their designs? If the characters of the holy Scriptures were of such immense size that each letter, when looked at near, would nearly fill our vision, we could see only one at a time, and we could not read; that is to say, we could not collect the letters into words and discover the sense of the whole. It is the same with the great features of the providence of God that have been delineated in the government of the world for so many ages. It is only the whole that can be intelligible, and the whole is too vast for a near view. Every event is a particular character, which is too great for the smallness of our organs, and which means nothing if it is separated from the others.

When we will see God as He is and see all the events of human life from the first to the last day, in all their proportions and their relations to the designs of God, then we will exclaim, "O, Lord, You alone are good and wise!" We judge the works of men only by examining the whole. Every part ought not to have all perfection, but only that which belongs to it in the order and in the proportion that pervades the whole. In the human body, it would not be well that all the organs should be eyes; feet and hands are also necessary. In the universe, we want the sun for the day, but we also want the moon for the night. It is thus we ought to judge of every part by its relation to the whole; every other view is narrow and false. But how insignificant are the designs of men when we compare them with the creation and government of the universe!

Let man, then, admire what he understands, and let him be silent when he cannot comprehend. There is nothing in the universe that does not equally bear these two opposite characters—the stamp of the Creator and the marks of the nothingness it came from and which it may, at any moment, be resolved into. It is an incomprehensible mixture of meanness and glory, of the frailty of the material and of skill in its conformation. The hand of God is displayed everywhere, even in the worm; and weakness and nothingness are discoverable everywhere, even in the most sublime geniuses. All but God Himself must be limited and imperfect; it may have more or less of imperfection, but it still must be ever imperfect; we must still be able to point out something in it of which we may say, "This is what should not be," or "This it does not possess."

Let us study this visible creation as we will. Take the anatomy of the meanest animal; look at the smallest grain of corn that is planted in the earth, and the manner in which its germ produces and multiplies; observe attentively the rosebud and how carefully it opens to the sun and closes at his setting—and we will see more skill and design than in all the works of man. What we call human art is only a feeble imitation of the great art that we call the laws of nature and that impiety has not been ashamed to call "blind chance."

Can we be astonished that poets have animated all nature, that they have given wings to the winds and darts to the sun, that they have painted rivers hastening to precipitate themselves into the sea and trees that reach the clouds to overcome the rays of the sun by the thickness of their foliage? These figures have been adopted even in common conversation, so natural is it for man to feel the power and skill with which the universe is filled.

Poetry has only attributed to inanimate things the design of the Creator. The language of the poets gave rise to the theology of the pagans; their theologians were poets. They imagined a power, a wisdom, in objects that are entirely destitute of intelligence. With them the rivers were gods and the fountains were naiads. The woods and the mountains had their particular divinities; the flowers were subject to Flora and the fruits to Pomona. The more enlarged our minds are when we contemplate nature, the more we discover of that inexhaustible wisdom that is the soul of the universe. Then do we see the Infinite Creator represented in all His works, as in a mirror, to the contemplation of His intelligent offspring. But some men have bewildered themselves with their own thoughts; everything with them turns into vanity. Through sophistical arguments, they lose sight of the truth that nature and simplicity would teach them without the aid of philosophy. Others, intoxicated by their passions, live unconscious of the presence of God. To perceive Him in His works, we at least ought to be attentive. Passion blinds not only the savage but also those who are surrounded by the light of religion.

It is thus we see men living in the world and thinking only of what gratifies passion and vanity, their souls so laden with the weight of earth that they cannot raise them to any spiritual object.

Whatever is not palpable—cannot be seen or heard or touched or counted—is unreal and chimerical to them. This weakness of the mind at last becomes incredulity and appears to them strength, and their vanity leads them to applaud themselves for being able to resist arguments that influence the rest of the world. It is as if a monster should boast of not being formed in the fashion of other men, or as if a blind man were to triumph at his incredulity about colors that other men perceive.

Prayer to God

O my God, while so many of Your children are unconscious of Your presence in this glorious scene of nature that You present to them, still You are not far from any one of them. You are near us, but we do not perceive You; our passions blind us.

Thus, O Lord, Your light shines in the darkness, and the darkness comprehends it not. You reveal Yourself everywhere, but men do not see You. All nature speaks of You and resounds with Your most holy name, but its voice is uttered to deafened ears—they will not hear. You are near them and within them, but they fly from themselves and from You. They would find You, O eternal and holy light, fountain of all pure and unfailing felicity, life of all true existence, if they would seek You within their souls. But, alas, Your good gifts that declare the bounty of the giver turn their attention from the hand that bestows them. They live in You without thinking of You; or rather, they die, for to be ignorant of You is death. You support them in the arms of Your mercy, and they are unconscious of it. It is because You are within them, in the temple of the soul into which they never enter, that You are hidden from them.

The order and beauty of the creation are like a veil that hides You from their weak vision. The light that should enlighten blinds them. You are too high and too pure to be perceived by their gross senses. The earthly-minded cannot comprehend You. It is a frightful darkness that envelopes the children of men when they can see only shadows, and even truth appears a phantom; when what is nothing seems all to them, and what is everything is as nothing to them. What do I see in all nature? God! God in everything and God alone! The one who does not see You has seen nothing. He is as if he was not, and his whole life is as a dream. Sorrow to the soul who has not seen You, that is far from God—without hope, without consolation! But blessed already are those who seek You, who thirst for You! Unspeakable is the felicity of those who rejoice in Your immediate presence, from whose eyes You have wiped away every tear, and whose hearts are filled with Your love and presence!

ON PIETY

How unspeakable are the blessings that piety bestows—pure and disinterested piety, piety that never fails, piety that does good in secret! It enables us to conquer our passions and our bad habits; it destroys our love of the polluting pleasures of the world; it touches our hearts with the salutary truths of religion. It protects us from the fatal snares that are around us. Will we be ungrateful for so many benefits? Will we not have the courage to sacrifice to piety all our irregular desires, however it may wound our self-love?

Let us examine ourselves, as in the presence of God, and see if such be our piety, and let us view the subject as it relates to God, to ourselves, and to our neighbor. These three relations will guide us in the following discourse.

Our Piety in Relation to God

Are we willing to suffer for God? Does our desire to be with Him destroy our fear of death? Do we love to think of God? Do we give ourselves up to Him? It is by asking ourselves these questions that we will ascertain the true state of our souls.

1. Are we willing to suffer for God?

I do not speak of a certain vague love of suffering that shows itself in words and fails in actions—of a willingness to suffer that consists only in a habit of talking magnificently and eloquently of the use of crosses, and shrinks from the slightest personal inconvenience, indulging instead in all the seductive pleasures of a sensual life. Neither do I mean a certain fanciful spirituality that is ever meditating upon resignation, patience, and the joy of tribulation while the whole life discovers a jealous self-love that is unwilling to suffer anything. True piety is not satisfied with offering to God a sterile faith; it would add the sacrifice of a humble heart, glad to suffer for Him.

In vain will you attempt to follow Jesus if you do not bear His cross. Dare you, can you, complain when you have His example to support you? Will not the faithful soul rejoice to suffer in imitation of Jesus and to show his love for Him with the hope of meriting the blessing that He has promised to those who weep? If I was seriously persuaded that the life of a Christian is a life of patience and self-denial, if in sincerity and truth I loved Jesus Christ who suffered and humbled Himself for me, should I be contented with *talking* of trials when I am called upon to *bear* them—with giving lessons to my neighbor and not applying them to myself? Should I be so impatient with the infirmities of others, so discouraged by obstacles, so disquieted by little troubles, so sensitive about human friendship, so jealous and intractable toward those whom I ought to conciliate, so severe toward the faults of others, so lenient and so backward in mending my own? Should I be so ready to murmur at the trials by which God would prove my virtue?

It is a scandal that might make the pious weep, to see men who profess to be followers of Christ crucified shrinking from sufferings and trials, men who would serve God with all possible convenience, who pretend to sigh after another life while they are clinging to all the delights of this life, who declaim with zeal against self-love while they take all imaginable precautions to save their own from the least mortification.

2. Are we willing to die to be with Christ?

Saint Augustine says that holiness of life and willingness to die are inseparable dispositions. "The love of this life and of another," says he, "cause an incessant conflict in the imperfect soul. Let not such persons say they wish to live in order to repair the past. If they examine their hearts, they will find that they cling to life, because they are not sufficiently virtuous to desire the pure joys of heaven." If we only feared the judgments of God upon our entrance into eternity, this fear would be calm and holy. The perfection of our love to God consists in our feeling an entire confidence in Him. If we loved Him as our Father, should we fear Him as our judge? Should we fly from His presence, should we tremble thus, when sickness warns us of the approach of death?

But there is a secret infidelity at the bottom of our hearts that stifles all these sentiments. We weep at the death of those we love, and we tremble at our own, as those who have no hope. Judging from our anxiety about this life, who would believe that we anticipated a happy futurity? How can those to whom religion has opened the path to another life, those whose hope is full of immortality, reconcile such substantial and glorious hopes with the vain enjoyments that fill their hearts in this world?

Our piety must be weak and imperfect if it does not conquer our fear of death. We must take a very confused and superficial view of the eternal resources of the Christian at the hour of death, and of all that he hopes for beyond this transient life, if our hearts do not kindle with joy at the contemplation of the moment when our sorrows will pass away and our felicity begin.

Let us each ask ourselves, "Am I ready to die? Let me not deceive myself by a false courage. Does the ardor of my love for God overcome my fear of death? Do I use this world as not abusing it? Do I regard it as a passing shadow? Am I unwilling to be subjected to its vanities? Is there nothing here that flatters my self-love and enslaves my affections, making me almost forget eternity? In fine, am I every day preparing for death? Is it by this thought that I regulate my life? And when the last hour arrives, will I be prepared for the fatal stroke? Will I not shrink from its approach? What will become of my courage when I feel myself between this world that is fast vanishing from my sight and eternity that is opening to receive me?"

Why is it that those who profess not to be lovers of life do not fear death less than others?

3. Do we enjoy the contemplation of God?

Do we feel a sincere joy when we pray to Him and when we meditate upon His presence? Prayer, says Saint Augustine, is the measure of love. The one who loves much, prays much. The one whose heart is closely united to God has no sweeter consolation than in communion with Him. He finds a positive happiness in being able to love Him, to speak to Him, to meditate upon His attributes, to adore His majesty, to admire His power, to dwell on His goodness, and to yield himself up to His providence. In this communication, he pours out, as into the bosom of a tender father, all the sorrows of his overflowing heart. This is his resource under every affliction; he finds strength and consolation in spreading out all his weaknesses and all his desires; and as our whole lives are full of imperfections, as we are never free from sin, we should always, in the exercise of prayer, ask pardon of God for our ingratitude and thank Him for His mercy.

Let us pray, then, but let us pray with all our duties before us. Do not let us make eloquent and abstract prayers that have no connection with the practice of virtue, but let us pray to become more humble, more docile, more patient, more charitable, more modest, more pure, and more disinterested in the performance of our duties. Without this, our prayer will be an illusion to ourselves and a scandal to our neighbor. An illusion to ourselves—for how often do we see a devotion that only nourishes pride and misleads the imagination? A scandal to our neighbor—for there can be no greater scandal than to see a person who prays unceasingly without correcting his faults, who comes from his orisons[4] neither less frivolous nor less discontented and anxious nor less selfish than he was before.

Are we resolved to give ourselves up without reserve to God? Do we consider His protecting providence our best resource, or do we have a timid anxiety concerning our own affairs that renders us unworthy of His care?

The disposition essential to the soul that consecrates itself to God is to desire nothing but in reference to His will. Why is it that so many good people undertake good works without any success? It is because they commence them without any sincere trust in God and without a complete renunciation of self. The thought of self is never entirely excluded.

They do not prefer the interest of God's work above their own ill-regulated inclinations and perverse fancies; a weak jealousy of authority and a desire of consideration contaminate the best things. In summary, it is because they wish to serve God with a security of benefiting themselves; they are not willing to risk their own glory, and they would be very unhappy if they were exposed to any misapprehension through their love for Him. Can we expect from these cowardly and mercenary souls the magnanimity and the strength that are requisite to promote the designs of Providence? The one who distrusts God is not worthy to be His instrument. God, as Saint Paul says, *"over all is rich"* (Romans 10:12), but it is *"unto all that call upon him"* and trust in Him.

Our Piety in Relation to Ourselves

But we will proceed to the second part of this discourse. What are our dispositions with regard to ourselves?

Let us examine ourselves upon these four questions.

1. Our zeal: Is it imprudence under the pretext of religion?
2. Our prudence: Is it earthly-mindedness?

---

4. *orisons*: prayers

3.   Our devotion: Is it the effect of natural temperament?
4.   Our charity: Is it but an amusement?

1. Our zeal: Is it imprudence under the pretext of religion?

Let every root of bitterness, said the writer to the Hebrews, be put away from you. (See Hebrews 12:15.) There is a violent zeal that we must correct; it thinks it can change the whole world. It would reform everything; it would subject everyone to its laws. The origin of this zeal is disgraceful. The defects of our neighbor interfere with our own; our vanity is wounded by that of another; our own haughtiness finds our neighbors ridiculous and insupportable; our restlessness is rebuked by the sluggishness and indolence of this person; our gloom is disturbed by the gaiety and frivolities of that person, and our heedlessness by the shrewdness and address of another.

If we were faultless, we should not be so much annoyed by the defects of those with whom we associate. If we were to acknowledge honestly that we do not have virtue enough to bear patiently with our neighbor's weaknesses, we would show our own imperfection, and this alarms our vanity. We, therefore, make our weakness pass for strength, elevate it to a virtue, and call it zeal—an imaginary and often hypocritical zeal. For is it not surprising to see how tranquil we are about the errors of others when they do not trouble us, and how soon this wonderful zeal kindles against those who excite our jealousy or weary our patience?

If our zeal is true, it will be regulated by Christianity. It will begin with us. It will be so occupied with our own defects and our own wants that it will find little time to think of those of others, and when conscience obliges us to correct our neighbor, we will be very cautious with regard to ourselves, following the advice of the apostle to rebuke a brother *in the spirit of meekness; considering thyself, lest thou also be tempted* (Galatians 6:1). Whatever is said or done with passion will not make our neighbor better.

Where do we see any good effects from harsh reproof? We must gain the heart when we would recommend religion, and hearts are won only by love and condescension. It is not enough to be right; it is dishonoring to reason to defend it with violence and haughtiness. It is by gentleness, by patience, and by love that we insensibly lead the mind to truth, undermine old prejudices, inspire confidence, and encourage one to conquer bad habits. When he who receives correction perceives that reproof is given with ill humor, his own is not subdued by it, and his self-love revolts at the mortifying lesson. *"For the wrath of man worketh not the righteousness of God"* (James 1:20).

2. Our prudence: Is it earthly-mindedness?

Our prudence—is it not an earthly policy, a blind prudence, that, the apostle says *"is death"* (Romans 8:6) and is not subject to the law of God? There is an absolute incompatibility between this sort of worldly wisdom and that of the true children of God. How many good works do we see arrested by considerations of mere earthly prudence? How many sacred duties are yielded to the imaginary claims of politeness?

Formerly, Christians despised the undeserved contempt of the world; now, they fear its judgments and seek for its favor. They regulate their conduct by its whimsical prejudices, and they consult it even on the holiest of subjects. They do this not merely so that they may avoid scandal, which is right, but in order to accommodate themselves to its vain maxims and allow their good works to depend upon its decision. What pains do we take to acquire consideration and confidence—what anxiety, what eagerness for reputation? When we serve God thus, we serve Him feebly. Our hearts are divided between Him and a thousand objects unworthy of being remembered before Him. We seek the glory of God, we really desire it, but it is upon certain conditions that destroy our best purposes. "We carry," says Saint Augustine, "a languid will to the practice of virtue, and thus our minds are flattered while our hearts are not changed."

Who is there among us who desires perfection as it ought to be desired—more than pleasure, more than reputation? Who is willing to sacrifice all that is incompatible with it? Henceforward, let our prudence be regulated by the Spirit of God; let it not be an earthly-minded prudence. Let us be prudent so that we may do good; let us be full of charity toward our neighbor but full of distrust concerning ourselves. Let us be prudent, but let our prudence be to promote the glory of God, to show the true dignity of religion, and to make us forget ourselves.

3. Our devotion: Is it the effect of natural temperament?

Is our devotion not the effect of temperament? The apostle, predicting the misfortunes with which religion was menaced, said, *"Men shall be lovers of their own selves"* (2 Timothy 3:2). This is what we see every day—men quit the amusements of social life, live in retirement and with strict regularity; but it is because their temperament is harsh and they prefer solitude. Others are modest and gentle, but this is the effect of weakness and indolence rather than virtue. There is but one gospel, yet each one adapts it to his own peculiar inclinations. We are commanded to do violence to our inclinations, but instead, we see people forcing religion to their own interests. I know that the grace of God takes various forms in different minds, but after all, the essentials of religion are the same, and although there are many ways of going to God, they all meet at one point. They all bind us to the obedience of the same law and hold us in an entire union of sentiment and practice.

Yet where do we see this admirable conformity? Everywhere we see men who disfigure religion by vain attempts to make it accord with their own caprices. One is fervent in prayer, but he is insensible to the miseries and weaknesses of his neighbor. Another talks much of the love of God and of self-sacrifice, while he is not willing to suffer the least contradiction. Another deprives himself of allowed pleasures so that he may indulge himself in those that are forbidden.

This woman is fervent and scrupulous in works of supererogation but faithless in the most common and positive duties; she fasts and prays, but she does not restrain her pride or the violence of her temper. Thus we see people who think that because they do what they are not commanded to do, they may dispense with what is required.

Far better is the simple obedience that finds the rule of life in the gospel and follows it without any of those extravagances that disturb its calm and celestial features. Place each virtue in its proper rank. Practice, according to the measure of your gifts, the most difficult virtues, but do not practice them at the expense of others. Charity and justice are the first of the virtues; why cherish one at the expense of the other? Be strict, even austere, if you will, but be humble. Be very zealous for the reformation of abuses, but be gentle, charitable, and compassionate. Do for the glory of God all that your love for Him prompts, but begin with the performance of all the duties of the situation in which you are placed. Without this, your virtues are only whims and fancies, and instead of glorifying God, you are a subject for the scandal of the world.

4. Our charity: Is it but an amusement?

Our charity—is it not an amusement? Our friendships—are they not vain and ill regulated? Is not Saint Chrysostom right in saying that we are more faithless to God in our friendships than even in our enmities? For, says he, there is a terrible law against him who hates his neighbor, and when we discover in ourselves the feelings of hatred and vengeance, we are shocked and make haste to be reconciled to our brother. But it is not so with our friendships. It seems so innocent, so natural, so conformable to charity to love our brethren that religion seems to authorize it, and thus we are not enough on our guard in forming our friendships, and they are often the result of whim or a blind prejudice.

Let us give everything its proper place in our hearts. Are our friendships regulated by religion? Do we love those friends more than others whom we can carry in our thoughts to God and who can themselves lead us to Him? Do we seek such with a real pleasure? Alas, how frivolous are our friendships! What loss of time in expressing feelings that often do not exist! How many useless or dangerous confessions! How many unjust preferences destroying the confiding affection and harmony of families!

I know that we are permitted to love those with more tenderness who possess distinguished excellence and those who are bound to us by the ties of nature and sympathy, but we must be sober and moderate even in these friendships. Let them dwell in the very bottom of our hearts, but there let them be controlled by a calm discretion and be ever kept in subjection by the general law of charity. Let them be outwardly expressed only so far as is necessary to show esteem and the cordiality and gratitude that we ought to manifest. We should never allow those movements of tenderness to escape us or indulge in those familiar caresses and expressions of partiality that may wound others. The most holy friendships should be restrained within these bounds.

Our Piety in Relation to Others

In the regulation of our conduct toward our neighbor, we are called upon to be gentle and humble, to act, and to suffer.

1. We must be gentle and humble.

The foundation of peace with all men is humility. God resists the proud but gives grace to the humble. (See James 4:6.) It is essential to men in their mutual intercourse to cultivate humility; pride is incompatible with pride, which is why divisions arise in the world.

Humility is still more necessary where we would promote the designs of God, which are to be supported only by the same spirit that the Son of God has Himself chosen for the execution of His great work, the establishment of religion. We must be ready to perform the most menial offices; we should not desire any distinction; we should be sincerely contented with obscurity and be willing to be forgotten by the world. We should esteem such a situation as a happy asylum. We should renounce in our hearts all desire of reputation for understanding, or for virtue, that might awaken a secret self-complacency and be a low and unworthy recompense for any sacrifices we may have made to the will of God. We should be able to say from our retreat what the prophet king said in the midst of his triumph: "I will humble myself yet more in my own eyes, that I may please You, O my God!" (See 2 Samuel 6:22.)

We must stifle all rising jealousies, all little contrivances to promote our own glory; all vain desires to please, or to succeed, or to be praised; the fear of seeing others preferred to ourselves; the anxiety to have our plans carried into effect; the natural love of dominion; and the desire to influence others. These rules are soon given, but it is not so easy to observe them. Our natures must be subdued by the grace of God in our hearts before we can, at all times, act with such simplicity and humility. With some people, not only pride and hauteur render these duties very difficult, but also great natural sensitiveness makes the practice of them nearly impossible. And instead of respecting their neighbor with a true feeling of humility, all their charity amounts only to a sort of compassionate toleration that nearly resembles contempt.

2. We must act.

During the short and precious time that is allowed us on earth, let us hasten to employ ourselves. While time remains to us, let us not fail to consecrate it to good works. For when everything else will have vanished forever, the works of the just will follow them, even beyond this life. For it is certain, according to the beautiful language of Saint Paul, that we have been *"created in Jesus Christ unto good works...that we should walk in them"* (Ephesians 2:10). That is to say, we should pass our whole lives in this happy employment.

Let us then do good according to the means that God has given us, with discretion, with courage, and with perseverance. With discretion, because, while charity extends its efforts for the glory of God, it also regulates its exertions by the nature of the work and by the condition of the one who undertakes it; it avoids disproportionate designs. With courage, for Saint Paul exhorts us not to become weary in well doing. (See Galatians 6:9.) With perseverance, for we often see weak and yielding spirits who very soon begin to turn back in their course.

We will find occasions to do good everywhere; they surround us. It is the will that is needed. The deepest solitudes, when we seem to have the least communication with others, will furnish us with means of doing good to our fellow beings and of glorifying the One who is their master and ours.

3. We must suffer.

Finally, we must suffer, and I will finish this discourse with one of the most important truths with which I commenced it. Yes, we must suffer, not only in submission to the will of Providence for the purification of our souls and the perfection of our virtues, but often for the success of those designs of which God has made us the instruments. Whoever desires to do good must be willing and must expect to suffer. You must arm yourselves with courage and patience. You must be willing to endure tribulations and trials of all sorts, which would overwhelm you if you were not supported by well-established faith and charity.

The world will blame and will tempt you; your friends and your enemies may appear to combine against your good designs. Those even with whom you are united to promote a good work may be a snare to you. Opposite humors and temperaments, different views, and contrary habits may cause you great suffering from those upon whom you have depended for support and consolation. Their defects and yours will perpetually clash in your interactions with them. If true charity does not soften these difficulties, if a more than common virtue does not sustain you under these bitter trials, if an unfailing and fervent piety does not render this yoke easy to you, you will sink under it.

ON PRAYER

Of all the duties enjoined by Christianity, none is more essential and yet more neglected than prayer. Most people consider this exercise a fatiguing ceremony, one which they are justified in abridging as much as possible. Even those whose profession or fears lead them to pray do so with such languor and wandering of mind that their prayers, far from drawing down blessings, only increase their condemnation. I wish to demonstrate, in this discourse, first, the general necessity of prayer; second, the peculiar duty of prayer; and, third, the manner in which we ought to pray.

God Alone Instructs Us in Our Duty

The teachings of men, however wise and well-disposed they may be, are still ineffectual if God does not shed on the soul that light that opens the mind to truth. The imperfections of our fellow creatures cast a shade over the truths that we learn from them. Such is our weakness, that we do not receive, with sufficient docility, the instructions of those who are as imperfect as ourselves. A thousand suspicions, jealousies, fears, and prejudices prevent us from profiting, as we might, by what we hear from men; and though they announce the most serious truths, yet what they do weakens the effect of what they say. In a word, it is God alone who can perfectly teach us.

Saint Bernard said, in writing to a pious friend, "If you are seeking less to satisfy a vain curiosity than to get true wisdom, you will sooner find it in deserts than in books. The silence of the rocks and the pathless forests will teach you better than the eloquence of the most gifted men." "All," says Saint Augustine, "that we possess of truth and wisdom is a borrowed good, flowing from that fountain, for which we ought to thirst in the fearful desert of this world, that, being refreshed and invigorated by these dews from Heaven, we may not faint upon the road that conducts us to a better country. Every attempt to satisfy the cravings of our hearts at other sources only increases the void. You will be always poor if you do not possess the only true riches." All light that does not proceed from God is false; it only dazzles us; it sheds no illumination upon the difficult paths on which we must walk or along the precipices that are about us.

Our experience and our reflections cannot, on all occasions, give us just and certain rules of conduct. The advice of our wisest and most sincere friends is not always sufficient; many things escape their observation, and many that do not are too painful to be spoken. They suppress much from delicacy or sometimes from a fear of transgressing the bounds that our friendship and confidence in them will allow.

The criticisms of our enemies, however severe or vigilant they may be, fail to enlighten us with regard to ourselves. Their malignity furnishes our self-love with a pretext for the indulgence of the greatest faults. The blindness of our self-love is so great that we find reasons for being satisfied with ourselves while all the world condemns us. What must we learn from all this darkness? That it is God alone who can dissipate it; that it is He alone whom we can never doubt; that He alone is true and knows all things; that if we go to Him in sincerity, He will teach us what men dare not tell us and what books cannot—all that is essential for us to know.

Be assured that the greatest obstacle to true wisdom is the presumption inspired by that which is false. The first step toward this precious knowledge is earnestly to desire it, to feel the want of it, and to be convinced that those who seek it must address themselves to the Father of lights, who freely gives to him who asks in faith. (See James 1:17.) But if it is true that God alone can enlighten us, it is not the less true that He will do this only in answer to our prayers. Are we displeased that we can only obtain so great a blessing by asking for it? No part of the effort that we make to acquire the transient enjoyments of this life is necessary to obtain these heavenly blessings. What will we not do, what are we not willing to suffer, in order to possess dangerous and contemptible things—and often without any success? It is not thus with heavenly things. God is always ready to grant them to those who make the request in sincerity and truth. The Christian life is a long and continual tendency of our hearts toward that eternal goodness that we desire on earth. All our happiness consists in thirsting for it. Now this thirst is prayer. Ever desire to approach your Creator, and you will never cease to pray.

Do not think that it is necessary to pronounce many words. To pray is to say, "Let Your will be done." It is to form a good purpose; it is to raise your heart to God; it is to lament your weakness; it is to sigh at the recollection of your frequent disobedience. This prayer demands neither method nor science nor reasoning; it is not necessary to quit one's employment. It is a simple movement of the heart toward its Creator, and a desire that, whatever you are doing, you may do it to His glory. The best of all prayers is to act with a pure intention and with a continual reference to the will of God. It depends upon ourselves whether our prayers be efficacious. It is not by a miracle but by a change of heart that we are benefited by a spirit of submission. Let us believe, let us trust, let us hope, and God never will reject our prayer. Yet how many Christians do we see—strangers to the privilege, aliens from God—who seldom think of Him; who never open their hearts to Him; who seek elsewhere the counsels of a false wisdom and vain and dangerous consolations; who cannot resolve to seek (in humble, fervent prayer to God) a remedy for their griefs, a true knowledge of their defects, the necessary power to conquer their vicious and perverse inclinations, and the consolations and assistance they require so that they may not be discouraged in a virtuous life.

But some will say, "I have no interest in prayer; it wearies me. My imagination is excited by sensible and more agreeable objects, and wanders in spite of me."

If neither your reverence for the great truths of religion, nor the majesty of the ever-present Deity, nor the interest of your eternal salvation have power to arrest your mind and engage it in prayer—at least mourn with me for your infidelity. Be ashamed of your weakness, and wish that your thoughts were more under your control. Desire to become less frivolous and inconstant. Make an effort to subject your mind to this discipline. You will gradually acquire habit and facility. What is now tedious will become delightful, and you will then feel, with a peace that the world cannot give or take away, that God is good. Make a courageous effort to overcome yourself. There can be no occasion that calls for it more imperiously.

The Peculiar Obligation of Prayer

Were I to give all the proofs that the subject affords, I should describe every condition of life so that I might point out its dangers and the necessity of recourse to God in prayer. But I will simply state that under all circumstances we have need of prayer. There is no situation in which we can be placed where we do not have many virtues to acquire and many faults to correct. We find, in our temperament, or in our habits, or in the peculiar character of our minds, qualities that do not suit our occupations and that oppose our duties. One person is connected by marriage with another whose temper is so unequal that life becomes a perpetual warfare. Some who are exposed to the contagious atmosphere of the world find themselves so susceptible of the vanity they inhale that all their pure desires vanish. Others have solemnly promised to renounce their resentments, to conquer their aversions, to suffer with patience certain crosses, and to repress their eagerness for wealth; but nature prevails, and they are vindictive, violent, impatient, and avaricious.

Why is it that these resolutions are so frail? Why is it that all these people desire to improve—they wish to better perform their duty toward God and man—and yet they fail? It is that our own strength and wisdom alone are not enough. We undertake to do everything without God; therefore, we do not succeed. It is at the foot of the altar that we must seek counsel that will aid us. It is with God that we must lay our plans of virtue and usefulness; it is He alone who can render them successful. Without Him, all our designs, however good they may appear, are only temerity and delusion. Let us then pray, that we may learn what we are and what we ought to be. By this means, we will not only learn the number and the bad effects of our peculiar faults, but we will also learn to what virtues we are called, and the way to practice them. The rays of that pure and heavenly light that visits the humble soul will beam on us, and we will feel and understand that everything is possible to those who put their whole trust in God. Thus, not only to those who live in retirement, but also to those who are exposed to the agitations of the world and the excitements of business, it is peculiarly necessary—by contemplation and fervent prayer—to restore their souls to that serenity that the dissipations of life and commerce with men have disturbed. To those who are engaged in business, contemplation and prayer are much more difficult than to those who live in retirement, but it is far more necessary for them to have frequent recourse to God in fervent prayer. In the most holy occupation, a certain degree of precaution is necessary.

Do not devote all your time to action but reserve a certain portion of it for meditation upon eternity. We see Jesus Christ inviting His disciples to go apart in a desert place and rest awhile after their return from the cities where they had been to announce His religion. How much more necessary is it for us to approach the Source of all virtue so that we may revive our failing faith and charity when we return from the busy scenes of life, where men speak and act as if they had never known that there is a God? We should look upon prayer as the remedy for our weaknesses and the rectifier of our faults. The One who was without sin prayed constantly; how much more ought we, who are sinners, to be faithful in prayer!

Even the exercise of charity is often a snare to us; it calls us to certain occupations that dissipate the mind and that may degenerate into mere amusement. It is for this reason that Saint Chrysostom says that nothing is so important as to keep an exact proportion between the interior source of virtue and the external practice of it; otherwise, like the foolish virgins, we will find that the oil in our lamps is exhausted when the bridegroom comes. (See Matthew 25:1–13.) The necessity we feel that God should bless our labors is another powerful motive to prayer. It often happens that all human help is vain. It is God alone who can aid us, and it does not require much faith to believe that—less than our exertions, our foresight, and our industry; it is the blessing of the Almighty that can give success to our wishes.

Of the Manner in which We Ought to Pray

We must pray with attention. God listens to the voice of the heart, not to that of the lips. Our whole heart must be engaged in prayer. It must fasten upon what we pray for, and every human object must disappear from our minds. To whom must we speak with attention, if not to God? Can He demand less of us than that we should think of what we say to Him? Dare we hope that He will listen to us and think of us when we forget ourselves in the midst of our prayers? This attention to prayer, which it is so just to exact from Christians, may be practiced with less difficulty than we imagine. It is true that the most faithful souls suffer from occasional involuntary distractions. They cannot always control their imaginations and, in the silence of their spirits, enter into the presence of God.

But these unbidden wanderings of the mind ought not to trouble us; and they may conduce to our perfection even more than the most sublime and affecting prayers, if we earnestly strive to overcome them and submit with humility to this experience of our infirmity. But to dwell willingly on frivolous and worldly things during prayer, to make no effort to check the vain thoughts that intrude upon this sacred employment and come between us and the Father of our spirits—is not this choosing to live at the sport of our senses and to be separated from God?

We must also ask with faith, a faith so firm that it never hesitates. The one who prays without confidence cannot hope that his prayer will be granted. Will not God love the heart who trusts in Him? Will He reject those who bring all their treasures to Him and repose everything upon His goodness? When we pray to God with entire assurance, says Saint Cyprian, God Himself is the One who has given us the spirit of our prayer.

Then it is the Father listening to the words of His child; it is He who dwells in the depth of our hearts, teaching us to pray. But must we not confess that this filial confidence is wanting in all our prayers?

Is not prayer our resource only after all others have failed us? If we look into our hearts, will we not find that we ask of God as if we had never before received benefits from Him? Will we not discover there a secret infidelity that renders us unworthy of His goodness? Let us tremble, lest, when Jesus Christ will judge us, He pronounces the same reproach that He did to Peter: "*O thou of little faith, wherefore didst thou doubt?*" (Matthew 14:31).

We must join humility with trust. "Great God," said Daniel, "when we prostrate ourselves at Your feet, we do not place our hopes for the success of our prayers upon our righteousness but upon Your mercy." (See Daniel 9:18.) Without this disposition in our hearts, all others, however pious they may be, cannot please God. Saint Augustine observes that the failure of Peter should not be attributed to insincerity in his zeal for Jesus Christ. He loved his Master in good faith; in good faith he would rather have died than have forsaken Him; but his fault lay in trusting in his own strength to do what his heart dictated.

It is not enough to possess a right spirit, an exact knowledge of duty, and a sincere desire to perform it. We must continually renew this desire and enkindle this flame within us at the fountain of pure and eternal light. It is the humble and contrite heart that God will not despise. Mark the difference that the Evangelist has pointed out between the prayer of the proud and presumptuous Pharisee and the humble and penitent publican. (See Luke 18:10–14.) The one relates his virtues; the other deplores his sins. The good works of the one will be set aside, while the penitence of the other will be accepted.

It will be thus with many Christians. Sinners, vile in their own eyes, will be objects of the mercy of God; while some who have made professions of piety will be condemned on account of the pride and arrogance that have contaminated their good works. It will be so because they have said in their hearts, "Lord, I thank You that I am not as other men are." They imagine themselves to be privileged souls; they pretend that they alone have penetrated the mysteries of the kingdom of God. They have a language and science of their own, and they believe that their zeal can accomplish everything. Their regular lives favor their vanity, but in truth, they are incapable of self-sacrifice, and they go to their devotions with their hearts full of pride and presumption. Unhappy are those who pray in this manner. Unhappy are those whose prayers do not render them more humble, more submissive, more vigilant over their faults, and more willing to live in obscurity.

We must pray with love. It is love, says Saint Augustine, that asks, that seeks, that knocks, that finds, and that is faithful to what it finds. We cease to pray to God as soon as we cease to love Him, as soon as we cease to thirst for His perfections. The coldness of our love is the silence of our hearts toward God. Without this, we may pronounce prayers, but we do not pray. For what will lead us to meditate upon the laws of God if it is not the love of the One who has made these laws? Let our hearts be full of love, then, and they will pray. Happy are those who think seriously of the truths of religion, but far happier are those who feel and love them. We must ardently desire that God will grant us spiritual blessings, and the ardor of our wishes must render us worthy of the blessings. For if we pray only from custom, from fear, or in the time of tribulation; if we honor God only with our lips while our hearts are far from Him; if we do not feel a strong desire for the success of our prayers; if we feel a chilling indifference in approaching the One who is a consuming fire; if we have no zeal for His glory; if we do not feel hatred for sin and a thirst for perfection—then we cannot hope for a blessing upon such heartless prayers.

We must pray with perseverance. The perfect heart is never weary of seeking God. Ought we to complain if God sometimes leaves us to obscurity, doubt, and temptation? Trials purify humble souls, and they serve to expiate the faults of the unfaithful. They confound those who, even in their prayers, have flattered their cowardice and pride. If an innocent soul, devoted to God, suffers from any secret disturbance, it should be humble, adore the designs of God, and redouble its prayers and its fervor. How often do we hear those who daily reproach themselves with unfaithfulness toward God, complaining that He refuses to answer their prayers? They should acknowledge that it is their sins that have formed a thick cloud between heaven and them, and that God has justly hidden Himself from them. How often has He recalled us from our wanderings! How often, ungrateful as we are, have we been deaf to His voice and insensible to His goodness! He would make us feel that we are blind and miserable when we forsake Him; He would teach us, by privation, the value of the blessings that we have slighted. Shouldn't we bear our punishment with patience? Who can boast of having done all that he ought to have done, of having repaired all his past errors, of having purified his heart so that he may claim as a right that God should listen to his prayer? Alas, all our pride, great as it is, would not be sufficient to inspire such presumption. If, then, the Almighty does not grant our petitions, let us adore His justice, let us be silent, let us humble ourselves, and let us pray without ceasing. This humble perseverance will obtain from Him what we could never obtain by our own merit. It will make us pass happily from darkness to light. Know, says Saint Augustine, that God is near to us, even when He appears far from us.

We Should Pray with a Pure Intention

We should not mingle, in our prayers, what is false with what is real, what is perishable with what is eternal, what is low and temporal with that which concerns our salvation. Do not seek to render God the protector of your self-love and ambition but the promoter of your good desires. You ask for the gratification of your passions—to be delivered from the cross that He knows you need. Carry not to the foot of the altar irregular desires and indiscreet prayers; sigh not for vain and fleeting pleasures. Open your heart to your Father in heaven so that His Spirit may enable you to ask for the true riches.

How can He grant you, says Saint Augustine, what you do not yourself desire to receive? You pray every day that His will may be done and that His kingdom may come. How can you utter this prayer with sincerity when you prefer your own will to His and make His law yield to the vain pretexts with which your self-love seeks to elude it? Can you make this prayer—you who disturb His reign in your heart by so many impure and vain desires, who fear the arrival of His reign and do not desire for God to grant the things you seem to pray for? No. If He at this moment were to offer to give you a new heart and render you humble and meek and self-denying and willing to bear the cross, your pride would revolt, and you would not accept the offer, or you would make a reservation in favor of your ruling passion and try to accommodate your piety to your humor and fancies.

Methods and forms of prayer, received from pious and experienced Christians, should be treated with respect; but we must not neglect the essential of prayer, which is an earnest desire that God, who knows our wants better than we do ourselves, will supply them. His Holy Spirit will teach us to pray and will guide us when we are in need of His aid. But what is most important is the persuasion that the simplest, most humble mode of prayer is the best, the most acceptable, and the most conformable to the words of the Son of God and the apostles. In such prayers, we find light and strength to fulfill our duty with meekness and humility in whatever condition we may be placed. Without this help, we will form good resolutions in vain; deprived of this interior support, we will be without strength in all the difficulties and temptations of life.

Advice on the Exercises of Prayer and Piety

Perfect prayer must be the love of God. The excellence of this prayer does not consist in the number of words that we pronounce, for God sees our hearts and knows all that we want. The heart asks only what God wills that we should have. He who does not desire with his whole heart makes a deceitful prayer. How few are there who pray! For how few really wish for the true riches—humility, renunciation of their own will, and the reign of God upon the ruins of their self-love. We must desire these blessings sincerely and in connection with all the details of life. Otherwise, prayer is only an allusion, like a pleasant dream to a wretched sufferer who thinks he possesses a felicity that is far from him. Still, we must not cease to pray, even when we cannot feel this true love and sincere desire; God looks into the soul and will see the desire to love Him.

When we are engaged even in the works of God, we may feel an inevitable distraction of mind, but we carry within us a flame that is not extinguished but, on the contrary, nourishes a secret prayer that is like a lamp ever burning before the throne of the Supreme.

When the divine light begins to illuminate us, then we have a clear vision of truth, and we immediately recognize it. We need not reason to prove the splendor of the sun; it rises, and we see it. This union with God in prayer must be the result of faithful obedience to His will; by this alone must we measure our love for Him. Our meditations ought to become every day more profound and intimate; divine truths should enter the substance of our souls and nourish and grow with it. We ought to meditate upon truth, and meditate at leisure, in singleness of heart, without seeking ingenious and abstract thoughts.

Let us do good, according to the means that God has given us, with discernment, with courage, and with perseverance. With discernment—for charity, while it seeks to promote the glory of God by imparting to man, has reference to the nature, the work, and the condition of him who undertakes it. It avoids disproportionate designs. With courage—Saint Paul exhorted us not to be weary in well doing. (See Galatians 6:9.) That is, let us not be wanting in true zeal and faith. With perseverance—for we see weak spirits, light and inconstant minds, soon turning back in the career of virtue. We will always find occasions to do good; they present themselves everywhere. It is the will to do good that is wanting. Even solitude, where we seem to have no means of action (even the solitude that allows the least action and affords the least communication with our fellow beings), still presents opportunities of glorifying Him who is their Master and ours.

THE SPIRIT OF GOD TEACHES WITHIN

It is certain that the Scriptures declare that *"the Spirit of God dwelleth in you"* (1 Corinthians 3:16), that He animates us, speaks to us in silence, and suggests all truth to us. We are so united to Him that we are joined to the Lord in one spirit. (See 1 Corinthians 6:17.) This is what the Christian religion teaches us. Those learned men who have been most opposed to the idea of an interior life are obliged to acknowledge it. Notwithstanding this, they suppose that the external law, or rather the light from certain doctrines and reasonings, enlightens our minds, and that afterward, it is our reason that acts by itself from these instructions. They do not attach sufficient importance to the teacher within us, which is the Spirit of God. He is the soul of our soul, and without Him, we could form no thought or desire. Alas, then, of what blindness we are guilty if we suppose that we are alone in this interior sanctuary, while, on the contrary, God is there even more intimately than we are ourselves.

You will say, perhaps, "Are we then inspired?" Yes, doubtless, but not as the prophets and the apostles were. Without the actual inspiration of the Almighty, we could neither do nor will nor think anything. We are then always inspired, but we are ever stifling this inspiration. God never ceases to speak to us, but the noise of the world without and the tumult of our passions within bewilder us and prevent us from listening to Him. All must be silent around us, and all must be still within us, when we would listen with our whole souls to this voice. It is a still, small voice (see 1 Kings 19:12) and is heard only by those who listen to no other. Alas, how seldom is it that the soul is so still that it can hear when God speaks to it. Our vain desires and our self-love confuse the voice within us. We know that He speaks to us, that He demands something of us, but we cannot hear what He says, and we are often glad that He is unintelligible. Ought we to wonder that so many people, even religious people, are engrossed with amusements—are full of vain desires, false wisdom, and self-confidence—and cannot understand it, instead regarding this interior word of God as a chimera[5]?

This inspiration must not make us think that we are like prophets. The inspiration of the prophets was full of certainty upon those things that God commanded them to declare or to do; they were called upon to reveal what related to the future or to perform a miracle or to act with the divine authority. This inspiration, on the contrary, is without light and without certainty; it limits itself to teaching us obedience, patience, meekness, humility, and all other Christian virtues. It is not a divine monition to predict, to change the laws of nature, or to command men with an authority from God. It is a simple invitation from the depths of the soul to obey and to resign ourselves even to death, if it be the will of God. This inspiration, regarded thus and within these bounds and in its true simplicity, contains only the common doctrine of the Christian church. It has not in itself, if the imaginations of men add nothing to it, any temptation to presumption or illusion; on the contrary, it places us in the hands of God, trusting all to His Spirit without violating our liberty or leaving anything to our pride and fancies.

---

5. *chimera*: an illusion or fabrication of the mind

If this truth is admitted, that God always speaks within us, then it is true that He speaks to impenitent sinners; but they are deafened and stunned by the tumult of their passions and cannot hear His voice. His word to them is a fable. He speaks in the souls of sinners who are converted; they feel the remorse of conscience, and this remorse is the voice of God within them, reproaching them for their vices. When sinners are truly touched, they find no difficulty in comprehending this secret voice, for it is that which penetrates their souls. It is in them the two-edged sword of which the writer to the Hebrews speaks. (See Hebrews 4:12.) God makes Himself felt, understood, and followed. They hear this voice of mercy entering the very recesses of the heart in accents of tender reproach, and the soul is torn with agony. This is true contrition.

God speaks in the hearts of the wise and learned, those whose regular lives appear adorned with many virtues. But such persons are often too full of their own wisdom; they listen too much to themselves to listen much to God. They turn everything to reasoning; they form principles from natural wisdom and by worldly prudence that they could have arrived at much sooner by singleness of heart and a docility to the will of God. They often appear much better than they are. Theirs is a mixed excellence. They are too wise and great in their own eyes, and I have often remarked that an ignorant sinner who is beginning in his conversion to be touched with the true love of God is more disposed to understand this interior word of the Spirit than certain enlightened and wise people who have grown old in their own wisdom. God, who seeks to communicate Himself, cannot be received by these souls who are so full of themselves and their own virtue and wisdom, but His presence is with the simple. Where are these simple souls? I see but few of them. God sees them, and it is with them that He is pleased to dwell. *"My Father will love him, and we,"* says Jesus Christ, *"will come unto him, and make our abode with him"* (John 14:23).

ON THE USE OF CROSSES

We find it difficult to believe in that almighty goodness that inflicts trials on those whom it loves. Why, we say, should it please God to make us suffer? Why could He not make us good without making us miserable? Doubtless He could, for He is all-powerful. The hearts of men are in His hands, and He can turn them as He will. But He, who could save us from sorrow, has not chosen to do it, just as He has willed that men should slowly grow from infancy to manhood, instead of creating them at once in maturity. We have only to be silent and adore His profound wisdom without comprehending it. Thus we see clearly that we can be virtuous, but only to the degree that we become humble and disinterested, trusting everything to God without any unquiet concern about ourselves.

We have need of all our crosses. When we suffer much, it is because we have strong ties that it is necessary to loosen. We resist, and we thus retard the divine operation; we repulse the heavenly band, and it must come again. It would be wiser to yield ourselves at once to God. It would be a miracle if the operation of His providence, which overthrows our self-love, were not painful to us.

Would it be less miraculous if a soul, absorbed in its own concerns, should in a moment become dead to self, than if a child should go to sleep a child and wake up a man? The work of God in the heart, as upon the body, is invisible; it is by a train of almost insensible events. He not only produces these effects gradually but by ways that seem so simple and so calculated to succeed that human wisdom attributes the success to natural causes, and thus the finger of God is overlooked. Formerly every work of God was by a miracle, and this precluded that exercise of faith that He now demands of us. It is to try our faith that God renders this operation so slow and sorrowful.

The ingratitude and inconstancy of our fellow creatures, and the misapprehensions and disgust we meet with in prosperity, detach us from life and its deceitful enjoyments. God destroys the delusions of self-love by the experience He gives us of our sinfulness and our numberless errors. All this appears natural to us, and thus our self-love is consumed by a slow fire, while we would have it annihilated at once, in the overpowering flame of a pure and devoted love to God. Yet this would cost us but little pain. It is an excess of self-love that would become perfect in a moment rather than by slow degrees. What is it that makes us complain of the length of our trials? It is still this attachment to self—the very thing that God would destroy. Why should we complain? The love of the beings and things of this world is our evil—and still more the love of ourselves. Our Father in heaven orders a series of events that gradually detach us from the earth and finally from self. This operation is painful, but it is the disease of our souls that renders it necessary and that causes the pain we feel. Is it cruelty in the surgeon to cut to the quick? No, on the contrary, it is affection, and it is skill. He would so treat his only son.

And thus it is with God; His parental heart does not wish to grieve us; He must wound us to the very heart so that He may cure its malady. He must take from us what is most dear, lest we love it too much, lest we love it to the prejudice of our love for Him. We weep, we despair, we groan in our spirits, and we murmur against God; but He leaves us to our sorrow, and we are saved. Our present grief saves us from an eternal sorrow. He has placed the friends whom He has taken from us in safety to restore them to us in eternity. He has deprived us of them so that He may teach us to love them with a pure love, a love that we may enjoy in His presence forever; he confers a greater blessing than we were capable of desiring.

There happens nothing, even to the sinner, that God has not willed. It is He who does all, who rules, who gives to all whatever they receive. He has numbered the very hairs of our heads, the leaves of the trees, the sands on the seashore, and the drops of the ocean. In creating the universe, His wisdom has weighed and measured the least atom. He is the One who, every moment, produces and renews the breath of life within us. He is the One who has numbered our days. That which most astonishes us is nothing in the sight of God. Of what consequence is it whether this frail house of clay crumbles into dust a little sooner or a little later? What do people lose who are deprived of those whom they love? Perhaps they lose only a perpetual delirium; they lose their forgetfulness of God and of themselves, in which they were plunged. Or rather they gain, by the efficacy of this trial, the felicity of detachment from the world. The same stroke that saves the person who dies prepares others, by their suffering, to labor for their own salvation. Is it not then true that God is good, that He is tender and compassionate toward our real sorrows, even when He strikes us to the heart and when we are tempted to complain of His severity?

Very soon, those who are separated will be reunited, and there will appear no trace of the separation. Those who are about to set out upon a journey ought not to feel themselves far distant from those who have gone to the same country a few days before. Life is like a torrent: The past is but a dream; the present, while we are thinking of it, escapes us and is precipitated into the same abyss that has swallowed up the past; the future will not be of a different nature but will pass as rapidly. A few moments, and a few more, and all will be ended; what has appeared long and tedious will seem short when it is finished.

It is this unquiet self-love that renders us so sensitive. The sick man who sleeps ill thinks the night long. We exaggerate, from cowardice, all the evils that we encounter; they are great, but our sensibility increases them. The true way to bear them is to yield ourselves up with confidence to God. We suffer, indeed, but God wills this suffering so that it may purify us and render us worthy of Him. The world forgets us, slights us, is ungrateful to us, and places us in the rank of those who have passed away. Is it astonishing that the world should be unjust, treacherous, and deceitful? It is nevertheless the same world that you have not been ashamed to love so dearly, and that, perhaps, you still love; and this is the source of your sorrow.

Almighty God, You alone can see the whole extent of our misery, and You alone can cure it. Give us, we implore You, the faith, the hope, the love, and the Christian courage that we need. Enable us ever to raise our eyes to You, the all-powerful—who will give to Your children only what is for their everlasting good—and to Jesus Christ, Your Son, who is our example in suffering. Raise our hearts, O our Father; make them like His so that they may be self-denying and may fear only Your displeasure and eternal sorrow. O Lord, You see the weakness and desolation of the creature of Your hands. It has no resource in itself; it lacks everything and seeks in You with confidence the good it cannot find elsewhere.

ON DAILY FAULTS

There are many faults that are voluntary, to a certain degree, though they are not committed with a deliberate purpose of disobedience to God. We often reproach a friend for a fault that he knows gives us pain and that he still repeats with this knowledge, although not with the design to offend us. We sometimes commit such faults toward God. They are, in truth, voluntary, because though we do not reflect at the moment, yet we have an interior light in our consciences that should be sufficient at least to make us hesitate before we act. These are often the faults of very good people. Small offenses become great in our eyes as the light from God increases within us, just as the sun, when rising, reveals to us the magnitude of objects of which we had only a confused idea in the night. As this light rises within us, we must expect that the imperfections we now discover will appear greater and more sinful, and that we will see, springing up from our hearts, numerous defects that we never suspected were there. We will there find weaknesses enough to destroy our self-love and to demolish to the very foundation the fabric of human pride. Nothing proves more certainly the real advancement of the soul than the power to see these imperfections without being discouraged by them. When we perceive an inclination to do wrong before we have committed a fault, we must abstain from it; but after we have committed it, we must courageously endure the humiliation that follows. When we perceive the fault before we commit it, we must beware of resisting the Spirit of God that is warning us of danger and that may, if we neglect it, be silenced within us and, in time, leave us if we do not yield to it. The faults of precipitation or of frailty are nothing in comparison with those that render us deaf to this voice of the Holy Spirit, who is beginning to speak in the bottom of our hearts.

Those faults that we do not perceive till after they are committed will not be cured by inquietude and vexation with ourselves; on the contrary, this fretfulness is only the impatience of pride at the view of its own downfall. The only use, then, to be made of such errors is to submit quietly to the humiliation they bring, for it is not being humble to resist humility. We must condemn our faults, lament them, and repent of them without seeking any palliation or excuse. We must view ourselves as in the presence of God, with all our imperfections upon our heads and without any feeling of bitterness or discouragement, meekly improving our disgrace. Thus may we draw from the serpent a cure for the venom of his wound.

Very often, what we would offer to God is not what He calls upon us to relinquish. What He demands of us is often what we most cherish; it is this Isaac of our hearts, this only son, this well beloved, that He commands us to resign. It is His will that we should yield up all that is most dear; short of this obedience, we have no repose. Who has resisted the Almighty and been at peace? (See Job 9:4.) Do you desire the blessing of God upon your efforts? Give up everything to Him, and the God of peace will be with you. What consolation, what liberty, what strength, what enlargement of heart, what growth in grace comes when the love of ourselves is no longer between us and our Creator, and we have made, without hesitation, the last sacrifice!

Never let us be discouraged with ourselves; it is not when we are conscious of our faults that we are the most wicked. On the contrary, we are less so. We see by a brighter light; let us remember, for our consolation, that we never perceive our sins till we begin to cure them. We must neither flatter nor be impatient with ourselves in the correction of our faults. Despondency is not a state of humility; on the contrary, it is the vexation and despair of a cowardly pride, and nothing is worse. Whether we stumble or whether we fall, we must think only of rising again and going on in our course. Our faults may be useful to us if they cure us of a vain confidence in ourselves and do not deprive us of a humble and salutary confidence in God. Let us bless God with true thankfulness if He has enabled us to make any progress in virtue—as if we had made it through our own strength—and let us not be troubled with the weak agitations of self-love. Let them pass, and do not think of them. God never makes us feel our weaknesses but that we may be led to seek strength from Him. What is involuntary should not trouble us; but the great thing is to never act against the light within us, and to desire to follow where God would lead us.

ON THE AMUSEMENTS
THAT BELONG TO
OUR CONDITION

We should not, it appears to me, be troubled about those amusements in which we cannot avoid taking part. There are some people who think that they should be always mourning, that they should put a continual constraint upon themselves and feel disgust for those amusements to which they are obliged to submit. For my own part, I confess that I know not how to conform myself to these rigid notions. I prefer something more simple, which I also think would be more pleasing to God. When diversions are innocent in themselves, and we enter upon them with a due regard to the condition in which we are placed by Providence, then I think we may enjoy them with moderation and in the sight of God. Manners more reserved and harsh, less complaisant and frank, only serve to give a false idea of piety to the people of the world—who are already too prejudiced against them and who believe that we cannot serve God but by a melancholy and austere life. Let us go on our way in the simplicity of our hearts, with the peace and joy that are the fruits of the Holy Spirit. Whoever walks as in the presence of God in the most indifferent things does not cease to do His will, although he may appear to do nothing of much importance. I believe that we are conforming to the divine order and the will of Providence when we are doing even indifferent things that belong to our condition.

Most people, when they wish to be converted or to reform, think more of performing some difficult and extraordinary actions than of purifying their intentions and sacrificing their inclinations in the most common duties of their situation in life. In this they are deceived. It would be better to make less change in the action and a deeper change in the disposition with which it is performed. When we are already pursuing an honest and regular life, it is necessary to make a change within, rather than without, if we want to become Christians. God is not satisfied with the motion of the lips or the posture of the body or outward ceremonies. It is our undivided love that He demands; it is an acquiescence, without any reserve, to His will. Let us carry this submissive temper, this will, inspired by the will of God, wherever His providence conducts us. Let us seek the Father of our spirits in those times that seem so vacant, and they will be full of His presence. The most useless amusements may be converted into good works if we enter into them with proper decorum and in conformity to the will of God.

What enlargement of heart do we experience when we act with this simplicity? We walk like little children led by a tender parent, not fearing where we may go, and with the same freedom and joy. When piety has its foundation entirely in the will of God, regarding neither fancy nor temperament, and is not induced by an excessive zeal, how simple and graceful and lovely are all its movements! Those who possess this piety appear much like others; they are without affectation and without austerity; they are social and easy but still live in perpetual subjection to all their duties and in an unceasing renunciation of everything that does not, in some way, belong to the divine order that always governs. In short, they live in the pure vision of God, sacrificing to Him every irregular movement of nature. This is the adoration in spirit and in truth that Jesus Christ has taught. (See John 4:23–24.) All the rest is the mere ceremony of religion, the shadow rather than the substance of Christianity.

You ask by what means we can retain this purity of intention in our engagement with the world while thus partaking of its pleasures. "We find it difficult," you will say, "to defend ourselves against the torrent of evil passions and bad examples among men, even when we place a continual guard upon ourselves. How then do we hope to resist if we expose ourselves so readily to its pleasures, which may contaminate and must dissipate even the mind of the Christian?"

I acknowledge the danger, and I believe it even greater than it is said to be, and I admit the necessity of great precaution against these snares. These are the safeguards that I would recommend: reading, prayer, and meditation upon the great truths of religion. Fix your thoughts upon some action or instruction of Jesus Christ, and when you feel convinced of the truth that you have been considering, make a serious and particular application of it for the amendment of your defects. If you are faithful to retire, morning and evening, for the practice of this duty, you will find that it will serve as a counterpoise to the dangers that surround you. I say morning and evening, because the soul, like the body, must refresh itself at stated times, lest it faint and become exhausted in its commerce with the world. But we must be firm against temptations from without and from within if we would observe those periods. We never need be so engrossed by external things, however good they may be, as to forget the wants of the soul. I am persuaded that, in following these simple rules, we will insure an abundant blessing. While in the midst of pleasures, we will be moderate, discreet, and self-possessed, without constraint, without affectation, and without the severity that gives pain to others. We will be in the midst of these things as not being there, still preserving a cheerful and complaisant disposition; we will thus be all things to all men. (See 1 Corinthians 9:22.)

Should we feel at times disheartened and discouraged, a confiding thought, a simple movement of heart, toward God will renew our powers. Whatever He may demand of us, He will give us, at that moment, the strength and courage that we need. This is the daily bread for which we continually pray and which will never be denied us. For our Father, far from forsaking us, waits only for our hearts to be opened so that He may pour into them the stream of His unfailing love.

AGAINST TEMPTATIONS

There are but two things that we can do against temptations. The first is to be faithful to the light within us by avoiding all exposure to temptation that we are at liberty to avoid. I say, all that we are at liberty to avoid, because it does not always depend upon us whether we can escape the presence of sin. Those who belong to the situation in life in which Providence has placed us are not under our control. The other thing is to turn our eyes to God in the moment of temptation and to throw ourselves immediately upon the protection of heaven as a child, when in danger, flies to the arms of its parent.

The habitual conviction of the presence of God is the sovereign remedy; it supports, it consoles, it calms us. We must not be surprised that we are tempted. We are placed here to be proved by temptations. Everything is temptation to us. Crosses irritate our pride, and prosperity flatters it. Our lives are a continual warfare, but Jesus Christ combats with us. We must let temptations, like a tempest, beat upon our heads, and still move on, like a traveler surprised on the way by a storm, who wraps his cloak about him and goes on his journey in spite of the opposing elements.

In a certain sense, there is little to do in doing the will of God. Still, it is true that it is a great work, because it must be without any reserve. His Spirit enters the secret foldings of our hearts, and even the most upright affections and the most necessary attachments must be regulated by His will. But it is not the multitude of hard duties or constraint and contention that advance us in our Christian course. On the contrary, it is the yielding of our wills without restriction and without choice to tread cheerfully every day along the path on which Providence leads us—to seek nothing, to be discouraged by nothing, to see our duty in the present moment, and to trust all else, without reserve, to the will and power of God. Let us pray to our heavenly Father that our wills may be swallowed up in His.

ON FIDELITY
IN LITTLE THINGS

Great virtues are rare; the occasions for them are very rare; and when they do occur, we are prepared for them, we are excited by the grandeur of the sacrifice, and we are supported either by the splendor of the deed in the eyes of the world or by the self-complacency that we experience from the performance of an uncommon action. Little things are unforeseen; they return every moment. They come in contact with our pride, our indolence, our haughtiness, our readiness to take offense; they contradict our inclinations perpetually. We would much rather make certain great sacrifices for God, however violent and painful they might be, upon condition that we should be rewarded by liberty to follow our own desires and habits in the details of life. It is, however, only by fidelity in little things that a true and constant love for God can be distinguished from a passing fervor of spirit.

All great things are only a great number of small things that have been carefully collected together. The one who loses nothing will soon grow rich. Besides, let us remember that God looks on our actions only for the motive. The world judges us by appearance, but God counts for nothing what is most dazzling to men. What He desires is pure intention, true docility, and a sincere self-renunciation. All this is exercised more frequently, and in a way that tries us more severely, on common occasions rather than on great occasions. Sometimes we cling more tenaciously to a trifle than to a great interest. It would give us more pain to relinquish an amusement than to bestow a great sum in charity. We are more easily led away by little things, because we believe them more innocent and imagine that we are less attached to them; nevertheless, when God deprives us of them, we soon discover, from the pain of privation, how excessive and inexcusable was our attachment to them. The sincerity of our piety is also impeached by the neglect of minor duties. What probability is there that we should not hesitate to make great sacrifices when we shrink from slight ones?

But what is most dangerous to the mind is the habit it acquires of unfaithfulness. True love to God thinks nothing small. All that can please or displease Him is great. It does not produce constraint and weak scruples but it places no limits to its fidelity. It acts with simplicity, and as it is not embarrassed with things that God has not commanded, it never hesitates a moment about what He does command, whether it be great or small.

Those persons who are naturally less exact ought to make an inviolable law with themselves about trifles. They are tempted to despise them; they have a habit of thinking them of no consequence. They are not aware of the insensible growth of the passions; they forget even their own most fatal experience. They trust in a delusive courage, though it has before failed them, for the support of their fidelity.

"It is a trifle," they say. "It is nothing." True, but it is a nothing that will be everything to you, a trifle that you prefer to the will of God, a trifle that will be your ruin. There is no real elevation of mind in having contempt for little things; it is, on the contrary, a result of too narrow views that we consider those things of little importance that have, in fact, such extensive consequences. The more apt we are to neglect small things, the more we ought to fear the effects of this negligence, be watchful over ourselves, and place around us, if possible, some insurmountable barrier to this remissness. Do not let us be troubled at this constant attention to trifles; at first, it will require courage to maintain it, but it is a penance that we have need of and that will at last bring us peace and serenity. God will gradually render this state pleasant and easy to us.

ON SIMPLICITY

There is a simplicity that is a defect, and a simplicity that is a great virtue. Simplicity may be a want of discernment. When we speak of a person as simple, we may mean that he is credulous and perhaps vulgar. The simplicity that is a virtue is something sublime; everyone loves and admires it; but it is difficult to say exactly what this virtue is.

Simplicity is an uprightness of soul that has no reference to self; it is different from sincerity, and it is a still higher virtue. We see many people who are sincere without being simple; they only wish to pass for what they are, and they are unwilling to appear what they are not. They are always thinking of themselves, measuring their words, recalling their thoughts, and reviewing their actions, from the fear that they have done too much or too little. These persons are sincere, but they are not simple; they are not at ease with others, and others are not at ease with them. They are not free, ingenuous, or natural; we prefer people who are less correct, less perfect, and less artificial. This is the decision of man, and it is the judgment of

God, who would not have us so occupied with ourselves and thus, as it were, always arranging our features in a mirror.

To be wholly occupied with others, never to look within, is the state of blindness of those who are entirely engrossed by what is present and addressed to their senses; this is the very reverse of simplicity.

To be absorbed in self in whatever engages us (whether we are laboring for our fellow beings or for God), to be wise in our own eyes, to be reserved and full of ourselves, to be troubled at the least thing that disturbs our self-complacency—this is the opposite extreme. This is false wisdom, which, with all its glory, is but a little less absurd than the folly that pursues only pleasure. The one is intoxicated with all that it sees around it; the other with all that it imagines it has within; but it is delirium in both. To be absorbed in the contemplation of our own minds is really worse than to be engrossed by outward things, because it appears like wisdom and yet is not. We do not think of curing it; we pride ourselves upon it. We approve of it, and it gives us an unnatural strength; it is a sort of frenzy. We are not conscious of it; we are dying, and we think ourselves in health.

Simplicity consists in a just medium in which we are neither too much excited nor too composed. The soul is not carried away by outward things so that it cannot make all necessary reflections; neither does it make those continual references to self that a jealous sense of its own excellence multiplies to infinity. That freedom of the soul that looks straight onward in its path, losing no time to reason upon its steps, to study them, or to contemplate those that it has already taken, is true simplicity.

The first step in the progress of the soul is disengagement from outward things so that it may enter into itself and contemplate its true interests. This is a wise self-love. The second is to join to this the idea of God whom it fears. This is the feeble beginning of true wisdom, but the soul is still fixed upon itself. It is afraid that it does not fear God enough; it is still thinking of itself. These anxieties about ourselves are far removed from that peace and liberty that a true and simple love inspires. But it is not yet time for this; the soul must pass through this trouble. This operation of the Spirit of God in our hearts comes to us gradually. We approach step by step to this simplicity. In the third and last state, we begin to think of God more frequently. We think of ourselves less, and, insensibly, we lose ourselves in Him.

The more gentle and docile the soul is, the more it advances in this simplicity. It does not become blind to its own defects and unconscious of its imperfections; it is more than ever sensible of them; it feels a horror of the slightest sin. It sees more clearly its own corruption, but this sensibility does not arise from dwelling upon itself. By the light from the presence of God, we see how far removed we are from infinite purity.

Thus simplicity is free in its course, since it makes no preparation, but it can only belong to the soul that is purified by a true penitence. It must be the fruit of a perfect renunciation of self and an unreserved love of God. But though those who become penitents and tear themselves from the vanities of the world make self the object of thought, yet they must avoid an excessive and unquiet occupation with themselves—which would trouble and embarrass and retard them in their progress. Dwelling too much upon self produces, in weak minds, useless scruples and superstition and, in stronger minds, a presumptuous wisdom.

Both are contrary to true simplicity, which is free and direct and gives itself up without reserve and with a generous self-forgetfulness to the Father of spirits. How free and how intrepid are the motions, how glorious the progress that the soul makes, when delivered from all low, interested, and unquiet cares.

If we desire our friends to be simple and free with us, disencumbered of self in their intimacy with us, will it not please God, who is our truest friend, if we would surrender our souls to Him without fear or reserve, in that holy and sweet communion with

Him that He allows us? It is this simplicity that is the perfection of the true children of God. This is the end that we must have in view and to which we must be continually advancing.

This deliverance of the soul from all useless and selfish and unquiet cares brings to it a peace and a freedom that are unspeakable. This is true simplicity. It is easy to perceive, at the first glance, how glorious it is, but experience alone can make us comprehend the enlargement of heart that it produces. We are then like a child in the arms of its parent; we wish nothing more, we fear nothing, we yield ourselves up to this pure attachment, we are not anxious about what others think of us, and all our motions are free, graceful, and happy. We do not judge ourselves, and we do not fear to be judged.

Let us strive after this lovely simplicity; let us seek the path that leads to it. The farther we are from it, the more we must hasten our steps toward it. Very far from being simple, most Christians are not even sincere. They are not only disingenuous, but they are false, and they dissemble with their neighbor, with God, and with themselves. They practice a thousand little arts that indirectly distort the truth. Alas, every man is a liar; even those who are naturally upright, sincere, and ingenuous, and who are what is called "simple and natural," still have this jealous and sensitive reference to self in everything, which secretly nourishes pride and prevents that true simplicity which is the renunciation and perfect oblivion of self.

But it will be said, "How can I help being occupied with myself? A crowd of selfish fears trouble me and tyrannize my mind and excite a lively sensibility." The principal means to cure this is to yield yourself up sincerely to God; to place all your interests, pleasures, and reputation in His hands; to receive all the sufferings that He may inflict upon you in this scene of humiliation as trials and tests of your love to Him; and to neither fear the scrutiny nor avoid the censure of mankind. This state of willing acquiescence produces true liberty, and this liberty brings perfect simplicity. A soul that is liberated from the little earthly interests of self-love becomes confiding and moves straight onward, and its views expand even to infinity, just in proportion as its forgetfulness of self increases, and its peace is profound even in the midst of trouble.

I have already said that the opinion of the world conforms to the judgment of God upon this noble simplicity. The world admires, even in its votaries, the free and easy manners of a person who has lost sight of self. But the simplicity that is produced by a devotion to external things still more vain than self is not the true simplicity; it is only an image of it and cannot represent its greatness. Those who cannot find the substance pursue the shadow. Shadow though it is, it has a charm, for it has some resemblance to the reality that they have lost. A person full of defects who does not attempt to hide them, who does not seek to dazzle, who does not affect either talents or virtue, who does not appear to think of himself more than of others, but who has lost sight of this self of which we are so jealous, pleases greatly in spite of his defects. This false simplicity is taken for the true. On the contrary, a person full of talents, virtues, and exterior graces, if he appears artificial, if he is thinking of himself, if he affects the very best things, is a tedious and wearisome companion whom no one likes.

Nothing, then, we grant, is more lovely and grand than simplicity. But some will say, "Must we never think of self?" We need not practice this constraint; in trying to be simple, we may lose simplicity. What then must we do? Make no rule about it, but be satisfied that you affect nothing. When you are disposed to speak of yourself from vanity, you can only repress this strong desire by thinking of God or of what you are called upon by Him to do. Simplicity does not consist in false shame or false modesty any more than in pride or vainglory. When vanity would lead to egotism, we have only to turn from self; when, on the contrary, there is a necessity of speaking of ourselves, we must not reason too much about it. We must look straight at the end. But what will they think of me? They will think I am boasting. I will be suspected in speaking so freely of my own concerns.

None of these unquiet reflections should trouble us for one moment. Let us speak freely, ingenuously, and simply of ourselves when we are called upon to speak. It is thus that Saint Paul spoke often in his epistles. What true greatness there is in speaking with simplicity of oneself. Vainglory is sometimes hidden under an air of modesty and reserve. People do not wish to proclaim their own merit, but they would be very glad that others should discover it. They would have the reputation both of virtue and of the desire to hide it.

As to the matter of speaking against ourselves, I do not either blame or recommend it. When it arises from true simplicity and the hatred that God inspires in us of our sins, it is admirable, and thus I regard it in many holy men. But usually the surest and simplest way is not to speak unnecessarily of oneself, either good or evil. Self-love often prefers abuse to oblivion and silence; and when we have often spoken ill of ourselves, we are quite ready to be reconciled, just like angry lovers who, after a quarrel, redouble their blind devotion to each other.

This simplicity is manifested in the exterior. As the mind is freed from this idea of self, we act more naturally. All art ceases, and we act rightly, without thinking of what we are doing, by a sort of directness of purpose that is inexplicable to those who have no experience of it. To some, we may appear less simple than those who have a graver and more practiced manner, but these are people of bad taste who take the affectation of modesty for modesty itself and who have no knowledge of true simplicity. This true simplicity has sometimes a careless and irregular appearance, but it has the charm of truth and candor, and it sheds around it—pure and innocent, cheerful and peaceful—a loveliness that wins us when we see it intimately and with pure eyes.

How desirable is this simplicity! Who will give it to me? I will quit all else; it is the pearl of great price.

DIRECTIONS FOR THE CONSCIENCE OF A KING

Selections

Composed for the Duke of Burgundy

It is commonly said that the private vices of kings are less injurious than the mistakes they make as rulers. For my own part, I boldly assert the contrary, and I insist that all their defects as men are of infinite importance to the community. Examine your actions, then, in detail. Subjects are servile imitators of their rulers, especially when the passions are concerned. Have you then set any example of a criminal love? If you have, your authority has given distinction to infamy; you have broken down the barriers of honor and decency; you have afforded a triumph to vice and impudence; you have taught your subjects not to blush at what is disgraceful. It is a fatal lesson that they will never forget! It would be better, said

Jesus Christ, to be thrown with a millstone round your neck into the depth of the sea than to cause one of these little ones to offend. (See Matthew 18:6; Mark 9:42.)

Vice is in itself a contagious poison. Human nature is always liable to the contamination; it is ever ready to break the yoke of modesty. A spark causes a flame. A single action of a king may produce an increase and succession of crimes through many nations and through distant ages. Have you not given any of these fatal examples? Can you think that your irregularity will be secret? O no! The crimes of rulers are never secret. Their good actions may be hidden; people are slow to believe them; but evil is believed upon the slightest suspicion. Have you discountenanced irreligion in its lightest expression? Have you manifested your indignation at impiety? Have you made it felt and left no one to doubt your sentiments? Have you never been influenced by a false shame that has made you blush for the gospel? Have you demonstrated by your conversation and actions your sincere faith and zeal for Christianity? Have you used your authority to silence impiety? Have you shrunk with horror from immodest levity, equivocal expressions, and all other marks of licentiousness?

Have you committed no injustice toward foreign nations? The poor wretch who, from extreme necessity, steals a purse upon the highway is hanged, while the man who unjustly subjugates a neighboring state is called a hero. The unlawful seizure of a meadow or a vineyard is regarded as an offense against God, but no account is made of taking possession of cities and provinces. To take a field from an individual is a great sin; to take a country from a nation is an innocent and glorious action.

Where do these ideas of justice come from? Will God judge thus? Ought we to be less just in large matters than in little things? Is not justice still justice when great interests are at stake? Should we not have some scruples about committing a crime against a million men, against a whole country, when we dare not injure an individual? All, then, that is taken by mere conquest is taken unjustly, and ought to be restored. A treaty of peace that is made from necessity, because one party is the stronger, is like that which is made with a robber who has his pistol at your head. Your enemy is your brother; you cannot forget this without forgetting all humanity. You have no right to do him any harm when you can avoid it. You have no right to take up arms against him except in extreme necessity. And in making a treaty with him, it is no longer a question of war or of arms but of peace, justice, humanity, and good faith. And it is more infamous to deceive in a treaty of peace with a nation than in a private contract with an individual.

From a Letter to the Duke of Burgundy on the Same Subject

Never let your high rank prevent the exercise of kindness to the most insignificant. Put yourself in their place, and this condescension will not lessen your authority or their respect. Study men always; learn how to make use of them without familiarity. Seek merit, though it should be in the most obscure corner of the world: it is usually modest and retired. Virtue cannot penetrate the crowd; it has neither eagerness nor presumption, and it allows itself to be forgotten.

Do not be subdued by the artful and by flatterers. Let them feel that you do not love either their praises or their meanness. Put trust only in those who have the courage to contradict you with respect and who value your character more than your favor. Let all the world see that you think and feel as a prince should think and feel. It is important that the good love you, that the wicked fear you, and that all esteem you. Make haste, then, to correct yourself so that you may labor successfully to improve others.

True piety has in it nothing weak, nothing sad, nothing constrained. It enlarges the heart; it is simple, free, and attractive. The kingdom of God does not consist in a scrupulous observance of trifling formalities; it is in each individual the performance of the duties that belong to his condition. A great prince ought not to serve God in the same manner as a hermit or a private individual.

Feeling as affectionate an interest in the happiness of the whole human race as in his own nation in particular, and being as true an enemy to persecution as he was a sincere friend to justice and equity, the following is the wise advice that Fénelon gave to the Chevalier Saint George when he visited him at Cambrai in 1709–1710.

Above all things, never compel your subjects to change their religion. No human power can force the impenetrable entrenchments of liberty in the human heart. Force can never persuade men; it can only make hypocrites. When kings interfere with religion, instead of protecting it, they enslave it. Grant to all religions a political toleration—not equally approving of all, as if you were indifferent, but patiently allowing all that God allows and endeavoring to lead men by gentle persuasion.

Study the advantages of the peculiar form of government of your own country and the sentiments you ought to cherish toward your senate. This tribunal can do nothing without you. Have you not then sufficient power? You can do nothing without their consent. Are you not happy that you are at liberty to do good and not free to do evil? Every wise prince should rejoice to be only the executor of the laws and to have a supreme council who can moderate his authority. The paternal relation is the true model for governments; and every good father acts in concert with his wisest and most experienced children.

ON THE
EDUCATION OF GIRLS

Nothing is more neglected than the education of girls. Custom and the caprice of mothers determine it altogether. A careful education of boys is thought necessary for the public good, though it is frequently as defective as that of girls. Women in general have feebler minds than men; the weaker the mind is, the more important it is to fortify it. They have not only duties to fulfill, but duties that form the basis of social life. Is it not women who are the blessing or the ruin of families, who regulate the detail of domestic affairs, and who, of course, govern what most nearly relates to man? Thus they have a decided influence on the happiness or unhappiness of those who are connected with them. A judicious, industrious, religious woman is the soul of her family. Men, who exercise authority in public, cannot, by their deliberations, affect the general good if women do not aid them. The occupations of women are not less important to the public than those of men; they have families to govern, husbands to make happy, and children to educate.

It is ignorance that renders women frivolous. When they have arrived at a certain age, without habits of application, they cannot acquire a taste for it; whatever is serious appears to them sad; whatever demands continued attention fatigues them. The inclination for amusement, which is strong in youth, and the example of persons of the same age who are devoted to pleasure, have inspired them with a dread of an orderly and laborious life. At an early age, they lack that experience and authority that would make them useful at home. They do not understand the importance of domestic occupations unless their mothers have taken pains to instruct them. In this state of uselessness, a girl abandons herself to indolence, which is a languor of the soul, an inexhaustible source of ennui. She accustoms herself to sleep a third more than is necessary for the preservation of health; too much sleep enfeebles her and renders her delicate, whereas moderate sleep, accompanied by regular exercise, would produce gaiety and strength, forming the true perfection of the body, to say nothing of its influence on the mind. When idleness and weakness are thus united to ignorance, there arises from this union a pernicious taste for amusements. Girls brought up in this idle way have an ill-regulated imagination. Their curiosity, not being directed to substantial things, is turned toward vain and dangerous objects. They read books that nourish their vanity, and become passionately fond of romances, comedies, and fanciful adventures. Their minds become visionary; they accustom themselves to the extravagant language of the heroines of romance and are spoiled for common life.

To remedy all these evils, it is necessary to begin the education of girls with their earliest infancy. At that tender age, when they are left to the care of weak and often unprincipled women, the deepest impressions are sometimes made—impressions that have an influence during life. Before children can speak, we may instruct them. They are learning a language that they will soon speak with more correctness than scholars acquire in the use of languages that they have studied at a more mature age. For what is learning a language? It is not merely crowding the memory with words; it is observing the sense of each particular word. The child, in the midst of its cries and plays, notices of what object each word is the sign. It makes this observation sometimes in considering the natural movements of bodies that it touches or sees. The minds of children have an admirable facility to receive impressions from images. Thus, you may give them, by the assistance of tones and gestures, an inclination to be with honest and virtuous persons and, by the different expressions of the countenance and the tone of the voice, inspire a dread of those whom they have seen angry.

I speak of these little things as important, for there can be no doubt that deep impressions can thus be made on the minds of children. It is desirable that instruction should not be forced on children, that everything should be avoided that tends to excite the passions, and that they should gently be deprived of whatever they desire with too much ardor. If the disposition of a child is good, we may thus render it docile, patient, firm, happy, and tranquil. On the contrary, if this early period is neglected, a child will become impetuous and irritable through life. The child's habits are form-ing, and the child's soul, which has no bias toward any particular object, easily turns to evil. At a more advanced age, when reason is developing itself, every word we say should tend to inspire a love of truth and a contempt for every kind of dissimulation.

We should never coax children; if we do, we teach them to dis-guise the truth, and they never forget it. We must lead them by reason as much as possible. They observe everything. We must accustom them to speak little. The pleasure we derive from playful children often spoils them. We teach them to say everything that comes into their minds, to speak of things about which they have no distinct idea. This habit of judging with precipitation, of speaking of things without understanding them, remains during the rest of their lives, and forms a very defective order of mind.

We must take care of children without letting them perceive that we think of them. Let them see that it is your love and their helplessness that makes you attend to them, and not their merits. Content yourself with forming them by little and little; even when you can advance the mind of a child very far without forcing it, you ought to fear to do it, for the danger of vanity and presumption always outweighs the advantage of that premature education, which makes so much noise. We must content ourselves with following and aiding nature. Children, being ignorant, have many questions to ask; we must answer them correctly and sometimes add little comparisons in order to illustrate our meaning. If they judge of anything without understanding it well, we must try them by difficult questions in order to make them feel their ignorance without discouraging them. At the same time, we must make them perceive, not by vague praises but by some decided mark of esteem, that we approve of them if, when they are in doubt, they ask an explanation of what they do not understand and then decide after reflection. In this manner, we may gently teach them to be truly modest. From the time that their reason begins to develop itself, we must guard them against presumption. You see, you will say that you are better able to exercise your reason now than you were last year; in a year more, you will know things that you are not capable of understanding now. If last year you had attempted to judge things that you know now, but of which you were then ignorant, you would not have judged correctly. We commit a great error when we pretend to know what is beyond our comprehension.

The curiosity of children is an inclination of nature that anticipates instruction. We must not fail to profit by it. For example, in the country they see a mill, and they wish to know what it is; we must show them how it is that corn is thus prepared for man. They perceive reapers; we must explain to them what they do—how corn is sowed and multiplied in the earth. If you are in the city, surrounded by shops where several arts are exercised, and different kinds of merchandise are sold, you must not be impatient at their questions. The questions are so many openings that nature offers you to facilitate instruction. Listen to them with pleasure. By this means, you will insensibly teach them how all those things are made that man uses. Thus, gradually, without a particular study, they will learn the best manner of doing things, and the just value of each. Such knowledge should not be despised, since every one ought to be secure against imposition in his expenses. I think it is desirable to use indirect teaching to awaken the attention of children. Let us mingle instruction with their plays. Let wisdom show herself to them at intervals and with a smiling face. Beware of fatiguing them by ill-judged exactness. If virtue offers itself to a child under a melancholy and constrained aspect, while liberty and license present themselves under an agreeable form, all is lost; your labor is in vain.

Never permit a child to be flattered by its attendants; we adopt the manners and the sentiments of those whom we love. The pleasure they find in the society of ill-bred people gradually induces them to tolerate what they should despise. In order to render good men agreeable to children, we should lead them to remark what is amiable in them—their sincerity, modesty, fidelity, discretion, and, above all, their piety, which is the source of all the rest. If they have anything in their manners unpleasant, say to them, "Piety does not produce faults. When it is perfect, it cures them." But after all, we must not obstinately endeavor to make them like good people whose manners are disagreeable.

It is important for teachers to know their own faults; ask your friends to point them out to you. Children are very nice observers, and they will often perceive your slightest defects. In general, those who govern children forgive nothing in them but everything in themselves. This excites in children a spirit of criticism and malignity so that when they discover a fault, they are delighted. You must guard against this evil. Do not be afraid of speaking before a child of faults that you have committed. If you see the child is capable of reasoning on the subject, say that you wish to set the example of correcting faults by correcting your own; your imperfections will thus be the means of instructing and benefiting your child, and you will avoid the contempt you would otherwise awaken.

At the same time, you will seek every means to render agreeable all that you exact. If you have anything tiresome to propose, show its utility. We must always present to children the attainment of an agreeable or useful object, and never attempt to govern them by harsh and absolute authority. As their reason strengthens, we should reason with them. An austere and imperious air must be avoided, except in cases of extreme necessity, for children are generally timid and bashful. Make them love you; let them be free with you; let them not hide their faults from you; be indulgent to those who conceal nothing from you. Do not be astonished at their failings but, on the contrary, pity their weaknesses. It is true that this treatment will impose less the restraint of fear, but it will produce confidence and sincerity.

We must always commence with a conduct that is open, gladsome, and familiar, without trifling. By this means, we learn to understand children and know their real characters; whereas, if we subject them to obedience merely to authority, we govern by fatiguing forms; we produce a disgust of virtue, the love of which should be our first object to inspire in them. A child of lively imagination dislikes virtue and study because he dislikes the person who speaks of them; and this severe education makes the child retain painful ideas of religion through life. We must often tolerate things that we wish to correct, and wait for the moment when the mind of the child will be in a state to profit by instruction. Never correct a child in anger; if you do, it will be perceived, and you will lose your authority. Watch for the best moment to correct your child. Do not tell of faults without leaving hope of improvement. We ought to consider that children are weak; their age renders them extremely sensible to pleasure, and we have no right to require from them more than they can give. When we speak to them of words and things that they do not understand, we often leave a dangerous impression of ennui and sadness on their minds.

Though we cannot, at all times, avoid employing fear in the government of unruly children, we must never use it until we have tried every other method. We should always make children understand why we make use of fear, for joy and confidence ought to be habitually cherished in them. Otherwise their minds will become dull and thus will lose courage. If they are happy, they will be irritated; if timid, they will be rendered stupid. Like all violent remedies, fear should never be employed but in desperate cases. When we punish them, the suffering should be as slight as possible but accompanied by every circumstance that can inspire the child with shame and remorse. Show the child how gladly you would have avoided coming to this extremity; show that you suffer also; speak before the child to others of the misfortune of being so deficient in reason and sensibility as to require chastisement. Omit your accustomed marks of affection until you see that the child requires consolation; make the child's punishment public or private, as you judge will be more salutary.

We ought to adapt general rules to particular circumstances. Neither men nor children always resemble themselves. What is good today is dangerous tomorrow. A plan of conduct that never varies cannot be useful. Forms should be used as little as possible in their lessons. We may impart instruction more useful than their lessons convey by our conversation. I have known several children who have learned to read as a play; amusing stories have been read to them, and they have gradually learned their letters. After this, they have been anxious themselves to go to the source from which they have derived so much pleasure. The greatest defect of common education is that we are in the habit of putting pleasure all on one side and weariness on the other; all weariness in study, all pleasure in idleness. Let us try to change this association; let us render study agreeable; let us present it under the aspect of liberty and pleasure; let us sometimes permit study to be interrupted by little sallies of gaiety. These interruptions are necessary to relax the mind.

We must acknowledge that, of all the difficulties in education, none is comparable to that of educating children who are deficient in sensibility. Children of lively sensibility are liable to terrible faults; passion and presumption lead them astray; but they possess great resources, and often return from afar. Instruction is in them a hidden germ that springs up and yields fruit when experience comes to the assistance of reason. At all events, we can render them attentive, awaken their curiosity, and make them interested in our instructions. We can stimulate them by a principle of honor. By contrast, on indolent minds we have no hold. All their thoughts are wandering; they are never where they ought to be. We cannot touch them to the quick, even by correction; they hear all, and they feel nothing. The best education will be thrown away if we do not begin at an early age to remedy this evil.

It is necessary to observe that, in some children, we are very much deceived at first. They appear charming, because the early graces of infancy throw a luster over all their conduct. Every trait of intelligence that we see in them surprises us, because we did not expect it at that age; every fault of judgment is permitted, and in our eyes it has the charm of ingenuousness; we mistake animal spirits for intelligence. Hence it is that promising children who are celebrated at five years of age fall into neglect and are forgotten as they grow older. Of all the faculties of children, reason is the only one on which we can depend; if we cultivate it carefully, it always grows with them. The graces of childhood pass away; vivacity vanishes; even tenderness of heart is often lost, for the passions and the society of men insensibly harden the young in their interaction with the world.

Try then to discover, through the graces of childhood, whether the character you have to form is wanting in curiosity and insensible to virtuous ambition. In this case, it is almost impossible for those who have the care of the child not to be disheartened by a labor that affords so little interest. We must hasten to touch all the springs of the soul so that we may awaken it from this slumber. Be careful not to fatigue it or to overload its memory; endeavor to animate it, and do not fear to show it all of which it is capable. Be contented with little progress, and notice its slightest success; excite its ambition; let it see the error of distrusting its own powers. Lead the child to laugh freely with you at his timidity; point out those whose natural character is as timid as his own but who have conquered their temperament; teach him, by direct instruction, that timidity and idleness paralyze the intellect, that men who have these faults, whatever talents they possess, are imbecile and degrade themselves. But be careful not to give these instructions in an austere and impatient tone, for nothing sends the feelings back to the heart of a timid child like harshness. On the contrary, redouble your efforts to awaken the necessary zeal by pleasures suited to the child's age and character. We must endeavor to give to children of this class a taste for improvement; we must let them pursue whatever may cure them of their disgust to study, and permit some infringement of rules, taking care that they do not go to excess. It is more difficult to create taste in those who have none than to regulate an incorrect taste. There is another sort of sensibility more difficult to awaken— that of friendship. From the time a child is capable of affection, it is desirable to turn his heart toward those persons who do it good. By the child's affections, we can lead him to do whatever we wish; we have a certain influence over him, if we know how to use it; we have only to fear for the choice he makes of his friends.

There is another class of children who are naturally indifferent, reserved, and calculating. They deceive their parents, only pretending to love them, and they study their inclinations in order to conform to them. They appear more docile than other children of the same age, who act without disguise, according to their humor. Their docility, which is a concealed selfishness, appears to be genuine, and their dissimulation is not discovered until it is too late to correct it. If there is any fault of a child that education can not cure, it is without doubt this; and yet it is much more common than we have an idea of. Parents cannot resolve to believe that their children lack feeling; and, as no one dares to tell them of it, the evil increases. The chief remedy is to permit children from the earliest age to discover their inclinations so that we may know what they are; they are naturally simple and confiding, but the slightest restraint will be likely to inspire them with a wish to disguise, and they will never recover their simplicity.

It is true that God alone gives goodness and tenderness of heart; we can only try to excite it by generous examples, by liberal sentiments, by disinterestedness, and by disapprobation of those who love themselves too well. Before children have lost their native ingenuousness, we must make them taste the pleasure of cordial and reciprocal friendship. Those who surround them, therefore, should be amiable, sincere, frank, and disinterested; the persons who have the care of them had better have other faults than be at all wanting in these virtues.

Parents should be at all times affectionate and disinterested in their manners toward each other; it is from their parents that children often learn to love self. We must also, in their presence, avoid all feigned demonstrations of friendship that are often substituted for a love that ought to be real.

But we more frequently see children enthusiastic than indifferent. They never see two persons disagree without taking a lively interest in one or the other side; they are always full of affections and aversions without foundation; they see no fault in those they like, no good in those they dislike. We must gradually teach them that we are acquainted with all the good qualities of the persons they love and all the faults of those they dislike. Do not press the matter; they will gradually see the truth. Then, lead them to think of their own mistakes, and show them how unreasonable they are disposed to be. Relate to them errors like these that have happened in your own youth. Above all, point out to them the mixture of good and evil that is to be found in human nature, in order to check the extravagance of their friendships and the violence of their aversions.

Never promise children, as a reward for their good conduct, either clothing or sweets; by doing this, you create in them two faults: in the first place, you teach them to estimate highly what they ought to despise; in the second, you deprive yourself of the means of establishing recompenses that facilitate your labor. Be cautious how you force them to study. You must have as few rules as possible, and for those few, you must have a good reason. Though we should fear to excite the vanity of children by flattery, judicious praise is very necessary. Saint Paul often employed it to encourage the weak. We may also recompense children by innocent plays, by walks, by conversation, by little presents of pictures, or by geographical charts.

Children are extremely fond of stories; we see them transported with joy or shedding tears at their recital. Choose some fable at once innocent and ingenious; show them the serious intention of the author. When you have related one fable, wait until the child asks for another; when his curiosity is excited, recount certain select passages of history, but leave off at an interesting part; postpone the rest for the next day, leaving him impatient to hear the end. Animate your recital by a familiar tone of voice, and make your characters speak for themselves. This delights a child, particularly if he considers it as a reward. If the child has facility of language, he will, of his own accord, wish to repeat it to another person. You can choose one of his attendants who will be anxious to hear the story; he will delight to tell it. Do not appear to remark his mistakes, but when he has repeated several, give him some general advice upon the manner of relating a story, which is, to render it simple, short, and correct by a choice of circumstances that will best represent the whole.

We must endeavor to give children a greater taste for sacred history rather than any other—not by telling them that it is more interesting but by making them feel that it is so. Lead them to remark the important events that are to be found in it, such as the creation, the flood, the sacrifice of Isaac, and the birth and flight of Moses. By this means, we will not only awaken the curiosity of children, but we will lay the foundation of religious knowledge, which consists of many wonderful facts. Recount to them, in detail, the history of Jesus Christ; select the most striking parts of the gospel—His preaching in the temple at twelve years of age, His retreat to the desert, His temptation, the multiplication of bread, Lazarus resurrected, and the entrance into Jerusalem. Describe His death and His rising from the tomb. All these events, managed with discretion, will fill the imagination and the affectionate heart of a child with lively images of all the remarkable events that have happened since the creation of the world. The child will see the hand of God forever raised to confound the impious and protect the just. But we must select, among these histories, only such as afford pleasing or magnificent images, so as to render religion beautiful, lovely, and sublime,

When in the presence of children, we should never laugh at anything that is in any way associated with religion. We sometimes indulge ourselves in ridiculing the devotion of a simple mind, but we commit a great fault in so doing. We should speak of God with seriousness and reverence, and never trifle upon sacred subjects. In matters of propriety, we must be careful before children.

As women are in danger of superstition, we must try to enlighten and strengthen their minds. We must accustom them not to admit things without authority. Nothing is so painful as to see people of intellect and piety shudder at the thoughts of death. A woman ought to know how to resist weak fears, to be firm in danger, and to feel that a Christian of either sex should never be a coward; the soul of Christianity, if we may so call it, lies in the disregard of this life and the love of another.

There are several faults that are common to girls who are brought up in indolence and timidity. They are incapable of a firm and steady conduct; there is a good deal of affectation in those ill-founded alarms and those tears that they shed so easily. We must begin by treating them with indifference; we must repress our too tender love, little flatteries, and compliments. We must teach them to speak in a concise manner. Genuine good taste consists in saying much in a few words, in choosing among our thoughts, in having some order and arrangement in what we relate, in speaking with composure; however, women in general are enthusiastic in their language. Little can be expected from a woman who does not know how to express her thoughts with correctness or how to be silent.

Girls are timid and full of false shame, which is a source of dissimulation. To correct this, we must lead them to discover their thoughts without disguise; when they are tired, to say so; we must not oblige them to appear to enjoy books or society while fatigued by them. When they have acquired the unfortunate habit of disguising their feelings, we must show them by examples that it is possible to be discreet and prudent without being deceitful. And we must tell them that prudence consists in saying little and distrusting ourselves more than others, not in dissembling speeches. Simplicity and truth excite more confidence, and succeed better, even in this world, than dissimulation.

What is there more delightful than to be sincere, tranquil, in harmony with our conscience, and having nothing to fear and nothing to pretend? By contrast, she who dissembles is always agitated and under the necessity of hiding one deception by a hundred others; and yet, with all these efforts, she never fails to be discovered; sooner or later, she passes for what she is.

If the world is deceived respecting some solitary action, it is not so respecting the whole life. Truth always peeps out at some place; they are often the dupes even of those they wish to deceive, for people pretend to believe them, and they think themselves esteemed when they are despised. At least, they cannot prevent suspicions, and what can be more painful to a wise self-love than to inspire doubt and distrust?

Teach girls to say little, and that little according to the occasion and the person they address. Let them be reminded that *finesse* always belongs to a mean heart and a weak mind; people are artful because they have something to conceal, and do not dare to appear what they are. Take notice of the evil of certain little artifices that are committed and the contempt that falls upon those who are guilty of them. From time to time, deprive them of what they have gained by art, and tell them they will have whatever they want when they ask for it openly. Pity their little infirmities in order to induce them to discover them; false shame is the most dangerous of all defects, and the first to be corrected, for it will render all others incurable.

Guard children against the subtlety that leads another into a deception while they appear not to have been the cause of the deceit themselves; teach them that there is more baseness in such refinements than in common art. Say to a child that God is truth itself— that it is trifling with God to trifle with truth, and that He has given us language to be used in speaking with precision and simplicity so that we may say nothing but what is just and true. We must, above all things, avoid praising children when they discover art in trifling. Far from appearing to think such things pretty and amusing, we should correct them severely. When we praise children for such faults, we teach them that to deceive is to be ingenious.

The education of women, like that of men, should tend to prepare them for their duties; the difference of their employments will, of course, render their studies different. It is the duty of a woman to educate her children—the boys until a certain age and the girls until they are married. How much wisdom is requisite to manage the mind and disposition of each child, so as to guide his intellects, manage his humors, anticipate the effects of his growing passions, and rectify his errors? How much prudence should a mother have in order to maintain her authority over her children without losing their friendship and their confidence? Surely the mother of a family ought to possess a religious, mature, firm mind that is acquainted with the human heart. Saint Paul attaches such importance to the education of children that he says it is by mothers that the souls of children are saved. (See 1 Corinthians 7:14.)

I will not attempt to specify all that they ought to know in order to educate their children well. To do this, it would be necessary to enter into an entire detail of their studies; but we must not omit the subject of economy. Women in general are apt to neglect it and think it proper only for the lower classes; those women, especially, who are brought up in idleness and indolence disdain the details of domestic life.

It is nevertheless from ignorance that the science of economy is despised. The polished Greeks and Romans took care to instruct themselves in this art. That mind is of a low order that can only speak well and cannot act well; we often meet with women who utter wise maxims yet, nevertheless, are very frivolous in their conduct. It is well to accustom girls from their childhood to have the care of something—to make out accounts and to understand the value of things and their uses. But we must be careful not to let economy lead to avarice. A reasonable mind desires, by a frugal and industrious life, to avoid the shame and injustice that are produced by extravagance. We ought to retrench in superfluous expenses only that we may have more to bestow in charity and friendship; it is good order, and not sordid savings, that enlarges our means. Do not fail to represent the foolish economy of those women who save a lamp while they are careless in their general expenses.

Attend as much to neatness as you do to economy. Teach girls never to allow anything about them to be unclean or in disorder; lead them to notice the slightest derangement in a house. Say to them that nothing contributes more to economy and neatness than keeping things in their proper place. This may seem trifling, yet it leads to very important consequences. For then, when anything is wanted, there will be no difficulty in finding it; and when it is done with, it will be returned to the place it was taken from. This exact order forms the most essential part of neatness. For instance, a dish will not be soiled or broken if it is put in its proper place as soon as it has been used. The carefulness that makes us place things in order makes us keep them clean. Joined to all these advantages is that of giving to domestics a habit of neatness and activity by obliging them to place things in order and keep them clean.

At the same time, we must avoid fastidiousness. Neatness, when it is moderate, is a virtue; but when it is carried to an extreme, it narrows the mind. Teach children that it is a weakness to be troubled because a dish is not properly seasoned or a chair is put in the wrong place. This fastidiousness, if it is not repressed, becomes one

of the most dangerous faults; it will cause common folks to be disagreeable and wearisome to them. We should teach them early that
we are not to judge anyone merely by his manners, and point out
to them people whose manners are unpleasant but who, nevertheless, have a good heart and a correct mind and are a thousand times
more estimable than they who, under an accomplished address,
conceal a bad heart capable of all kinds of baseness and dissimulation. Say to them that those who are apt to feel a disgust at everything are usually weak. There is no man from whose conversation
we may not draw some good, and though we should choose the best
when we have the freedom of choice, yet we may be consoled when
we have not; we may lead people to speak of those subjects with
which they are acquainted, and thus derive some instruction from
the most ignorant.

The science of teaching others to serve us is not a slight one;
we must choose servants who have principle and religion; we must
understand their different duties, the time and the labor that ought
to be given to each thing, the manner of doing it well, and what is
necessary to do it with. For instance, you might blame a servant
for not having cooked a dish sooner than it was possible to do it, or
you would be in danger of being cheated by your servant from your
ignorance of the quantity necessary to use in doing a thing.

We must learn to understand the temper and to manage the
minds of our domestics. It is certainly necessary that we should have
authority, for the less reasonable men are, so much the more necessary is it that fear should restrain them. But we must remember
that they are our brethren in Jesus Christ, and that we should not
use authority until persuasion has failed. Endeavour to make your
servants love you without being familiar with them; do not enter
into conversation with them but speak to them often with sympathy and affection of their wants. Let them be certain of your advice
and your compassion. Do not reprove them harshly for their faults,
and do not appear offended or astonished at them while there is
any hope that they can be corrected. Speak to them with gentleness

and, with reason, submit to some neglects of service in order to convince them that you do not find fault from impatience or temper.

In regard to reading, I should permit a girl to read books of history and select works of eloquence and poetry, provided her judgment was sufficiently formed to bear the latter. In the education of a young girl, we should consult her condition and the place where she is to pass her life. Do not permit her to indulge hopes above her situation or her fortune; expecting too much has been the cause of much sorrow. If a girl is to live in the country, her mind should be formed for the pleasures of the country, and she should not be permitted to imbibe a taste for the city. If she is in a middling condition in the city, do not permit her to associate with those of a higher rank than herself. With respect to dress, we must endeavor to inspire girls with moderation. True wisdom consists in never displaying in our dress or our equipage anything remarkable; let there be nothing in their dress like affectation. We must endeavor to inspire them with compassion for the poor, and show them the sin of those who live only for themselves and refuse to give to those who suffer.

But the most important thing is to gain the heart of your daughter. Seek for her companions who will not injure her; furnish her with amusements that will not disgust her with the serious employments that occupy her the rest of the day. Endeavor to make her love God; do not let her regard Him as an inexorable judge who is watching to censure her. Let her learn to think of Him as a tender and compassionate Father. Do not let her regard prayer as a fatiguing constraint of the mind, but teach her to turn her thoughts inward to find God there. His kingdom is within us. Teach her to confess her faults to God, to represent her wants to Him, and to acquire the habit of acting always as in His presence, of being animated in the performance of duty by the spirit of love, and of placing all her confidence in Him.

III

LETTERS OF FÉNELON

From "The Spiritual Letters"

LETTER 1

Advice to a Man of the World Who Desired to Become Religious

I am greatly pleased at the kindness of heart with which you received the letter I had the honor to write to you. It must be the Spirit of God that has given you this thirst for truth and desire of assistance in your great work. I will be most happy to aid you. The more you seek for God, the nearer He will be to you; every step that you take toward Him will bring you peace and consolation.

Christian perfection, which people have a sort of dread of because of the idea that it imposes gloom and constraint, is not perfection except as it increases benevolence. We do not consider it constraint to do those things that we love to do. We find a pleasure in sacrificing ourselves to anyone whom we truly love. Thus, the more we advance in perfection, the more willing we are to follow its Author. What do we desire better than to be always satisfied and to be as well contented with crosses as with their opposite pleasures?

This is a contentment that you will never find in yielding yourself up to your passions, and it will never fail you if you give yourself up to God. It is true that this is not a contentment that flatters and excites like profane pleasures, but it is nevertheless genuine contentment, and far superior to what the world can give, for sinners ever desire what they cannot obtain. It is a quiet and sober peace, but the soul prefers it to the intoxication of passion. It is a peace in which we are in harmony with ourselves, a peace that is never disturbed but by our own unfaithfulness. As the world cannot give it, it cannot deprive us of it. If you doubt it, try it; *"O taste and see that the Lord is good"* (Psalm 34:8).

You will do well to regulate your time so that you may have every day a little leisure for reading, meditation, and prayer in order to review your defects, to study your duties, and to hold communion with God. You will be happy when a true love of Him will make this duty *easy.* When we love God, we do not ask what we should say to Him. We have no difficulty in conversing with a friend. Our hearts are ever open to Him. We do not think what we should say to Him, but we say it without reflection. We cannot be reserved. Even when we have nothing to say to Him, we are satisfied with being with Him. Oh, how much better are we sustained by love than by fear! Fear enslaves, constrains, and troubles us; but love persuades, consoles, and animates us; it possesses our whole souls and makes us desire goodness for its own sake.

It is true that the fear of the judgments of God is necessary to keep the passions under restraint; but if we must begin by fear that makes the flesh tremble, let us hasten to that love that consoles the spirit. Oh, how kind and faithful a friend will God be to those who enter into a sincere and constant friendship with Him!

The most important thing, if you really wish to be a religious man, is to distrust yourself, after so many proofs of your weakness, and to renounce immediately those companions who might lead you from the right path.

If you wish to love God, why should you wish to pass your life in friendship with those who do not love Him and who slight His love? Why are you not satisfied with the society of those who will confirm and strengthen your love for Him?

I do not wish that you should break off entirely your connections to all those persons with whom politeness requires you to associate, and still less do I wish you to neglect any of the duties of your station. But I refer to those connections that are voluntary and that may contaminate the heart and insensibly weaken your best resolutions—intimacies with the vain and foolish, and the company of those who despise piety and tempt you to a dangerous dissipation. These things are dangerous for the most confirmed in virtue, and of course they are still more pernicious for those who have taken only the first steps in the right path, from which it is so natural for them to turn aside.

I acknowledge that you ought not to present before the public a scene of ostentatious conversion, which might produce ill-natured remarks. True piety never demands these remonstrations. Two things only are necessary: one is not to set a bad example, so that we may never have to blush for the religion of Jesus; the other is to do, without affectation and without éclat[6], whatever a sincere love to God demands.

---

6. *éclat*: ostentatious display

LETTER 2

To One Who Was Undecided about a Religious Life

You may think me forward, but I cannot be reserved with you, although I have not the honor of an acquaintance with you. The knowledge that has been communicated to me of the situation of your heart affects me so deeply that it leads me to set aside forms. Your friends, who are also mine, have assured you of the sincerity of my interest in you. I can hardly realize a more perfect joy than to have you with me for some days.

In the meantime, I cannot avoid saying to you that we ought to yield ourselves up to God when He thus invites us to Himself. Do we deliberate so long when the world presents to us the seductions of pleasure and passion? Have we thus hesitated? Have we resisted evil as we resist good? Is it a question whether we will be deluded, corrupted, and lost—whether we will act against the most sacred convictions of the heart and the understanding? In seeking vanities and the pleasures of sense, we are not afraid of going too far. We decide immediately, and we yield ourselves up without reserve.

Is it a question of whether we will believe that an all-wise and all-powerful hand has made us, since we have not made ourselves? Is it a question whether we will acknowledge that we owe all to Him from whom we have received everything, and who has made us for Himself? We begin to hesitate, to deliberate, and to find subtle doubts upon the simplest and clearest things; we are even ashamed of being grateful to Him, and we dare not let the world see that we are willing to serve Him. In a word, we are as timid, as irreso-lute, and as scrupulous in the cause of virtue as we are unhesitating, bold, and decided in that of vice.

I ask but one thing of you, which is that you would follow in simplicity the bent of your own mind for goodness, as you have for-merly followed your earthly passions in the pursuit of evil.

Whenever you examine the proofs of our religion, you will find that no solid arguments can be opposed to it, and that those who contend against it do it only so that they may be free from its restraints. Thus, they refuse to obey God so that they may be devoted to self. Is this, in good faith, wise or just? Are so many deliberations necessary to conclude that He has not made us for ourselves but for Him? In serving Him, what do we risk? We will do, as before, all that is really honest and innocent. We will have, perhaps, the same duties to fulfill and the same sorrow to endure patiently. But we will have the infinite consolation of loving Him who is the sovereign good. We will labor, and we will suffer for Him who is our true and perfect friend and who will recompense us a hundredfold in this life, even by the peace that He will shed upon our souls. And we will add to this the anticipation of a life of eternal felicity, compared with which this life is a slow death.

Believe, then, your own heart, to which God, whom it has so long forgotten, is now speaking in love, notwithstanding its ingrati-tude. Consult the good, those whom you know to be sincere. Ask them what suffering comes from serving God. Learn from them whether they repent of their choice or whether they think they were rash and credulous in their conversion. They have been in the world as you have; ask them if they regret quitting it, and if the drunkenness of Babylon is sweeter than the peace of Zion. No; whatever we may endure in the Christian life, we can never lose that peace of mind that reconciles us to all we suffer and makes us cease to desire what we are deprived of.

Does the world bestow as much? You are acquainted with it. Are those who are devoted to it satisfied with what they have and not desirous of what they have not? Do they do everything from love and from their hearts? What do you fear? To quit what you will leave very soon, and what is leaving you every moment, and what can never fill your heart, which turns away from it with a mortal languor—your heart, which contains within itself a melancholy void, a secret reproach of conscience, and a sense of the nothingness of that by which you have been deluded?

Oh, what do you fear? To find a virtue too pure to imitate, a God too good to love, an attraction in goodness that will not leave you free to follow earthly vanities? What do you fear? To become too humble, too much detached from self, too pure, too just, too reasonable, too grateful to your Father in heaven? Oh, fear nothing so much as this unjust fear and this foolish wisdom of the world that deliberates between God and self, between virtue and vice, between gratitude and ingratitude, between life and death.

All that the most extravagant lovers have said in the delirium of passion is in one sense true. Not to love is not to live. The wildest passions that have transported mankind have been only the true love misplaced and wandering from that center to which it naturally tends. God has made us for Himself. He has kindled a flame in the bottom of our hearts that should ever burn like a lamp for Him who lighted it, and all other life is like death. We ought then to love.

But what should we love? That which we cannot love sincerely, that which is not lovely, that which vanishes as we would grasp it? What should we love in the world? Men, who are as great hypocrites in honesty as they accuse religious men of being in devotion; an honorable name, that perhaps we cannot keep, and that would not satisfy our hearts if we could; the esteem of ignorant persons, whom we perhaps individually despise? What will you love? This mortal body, which debases your mind and subjects your heart to the pains of its own diseases and to death? What will you do, then? Will you not love anything? Will you live without the soul of existence? Will you not love God, who desires that you should love Him, and who wishes you to give yourself to Him so that He may restore you to Himself? Do you fear, with this treasure, that you can want anything? Can you think that the infinite Creator cannot fill and satisfy your soul? Distrust yourself and all created beings; they are all nothing and cannot satisfy the heart of man, which was made for the love of God. But never doubt Him who is the sole good and who mercifully fills your heart with dissatisfaction toward all other things so that it may be constrained to return to Him.

LETTER 3

To the Same Person

Although I have not heard from you, I cannot forget you or relinquish the privilege you have given me. Suffer me then, I beg you, to represent to you how culpable you will be if you resist the truths and the strong feelings that God has awakened in your heart. It would be resisting His Holy Spirit. You cannot doubt the worthlessness of the world or its insufficiency to make you happy or the illusive nature of its flatteries. You acknowledge the rights of the Creator over the creature, and how much more inexcusable is ingratitude to Him than to man?

You recognize the truth that there is a God in the wisdom that shines in all His works and in the virtues with which He inspires those who love Him. What can you oppose to such touching truths? Is it not a real indocility of heart that produces this irresolution?

We are afraid of the yoke; this is the true leaven of unbelief. We try to persuade ourselves that we do not believe enough, and that, being in this state of doubt, we cannot take any steps in a religious life but with precaution, as if there were danger of soon retracting. What have you, in reality, to oppose to the truths of religion? Nothing but a fear of constraint and of being obliged to lead a serious life and of being led farther than you wish in the road to perfection. It is because you see the sacrifices that it demands that you are afraid of religion.

But permit me to say that you know not all its delights. You perceive what it deprives you of, but you do not see what it bestows. You exaggerate its sacrifices without looking at its consolations. It leaves no void in the heart. If it constrains your inclinations, the love with which it will inspire you will give you a relish for truth and virtue far superior to all your ill-regulated tastes. What do you expect from it? That it will perform a miracle to convert you? Even a miracle could not take from you this irresolution of self-love that fears a sacrifice. What will you gain by reasonings without end while your conscience declares the right that God has over you? Arguments will not cure the wound in your heart; you do not reason for the sake of conviction and action but so that you may find doubts and excuses and thereby retain your self-love.

You deserve that God should leave you to yourself, as a punishment for so long a resistance. But He loves you more than you know how to love yourself; He follows you with His mercy, and He troubles your heart to subdue it. Yield yourself to Him, and finish this dangerous irresolution. This hesitation between two courses is, in fact, a choice; it is the secret, lurking desire of the heart in the illusion of self-love, fearing to yield itself up, and ready to fly from the restraints that religion imposes.

Pardon the liberties I take, but I cannot moderate the zeal with which your confidence has inspired me.

LETTER 4

To the Duke de Cheveruse, on the Operations of the Divine Spirit in the Soul

I have given my attention to the difficulty you state of discriminating between the operations of the Spirit of God and our own natural understanding. We cannot have a precise and certain rule upon this subject within us. We have only an exterior guide for our actions, which is conformity to the precepts, counsels, and graces of Christianity. If we had, in addition to this, the means of distinguishing with certainty the divine influence from the operation of our natural powers, we should then be endowed with a sort of sanctity and infallibility that would amount to inspiration. This is exactly opposed to the uncertainty of faith and to a state of pilgrimage.

We ought not to seek what our present condition does not permit us to obtain; I mean a certain rule to decide when we are moved by a divine influence and when it is our nature imitating it.

On the other hand, it is of the utmost importance in our conduct, as a protection against illusion, to discern this difference and to have a certain rule for judging. We must, it is said, obey the divine influence; not to do it is to resist God, to constrain the Holy Spirit, and to turn away from that perfection to which we are called.

But how will we follow this divine guide if we have no certain rule by which to distinguish Him from the operations of our own minds? A want of certainty upon this subject leaves us in continual danger of acting contrarily to what we really desire, of being influenced by natural inclination when we desire to be guided by the Spirit of God. This is the difficulty; let us seek the remedy.

These doubts can never relate, as I have before observed, to those things that are forbidden by the precepts, the commands, and the charities of our religion. This holy influence not only can never lead us to violate the direct instructions but can never teach us to neglect any of the minor duties recommended in the gospel. Thus we see that there is no question about an entire purity and perfection of manners in the case. The question must be, between two right actions, to know which is the prompting of this inward teacher.

It is true that in this choice, we have no certainty of internal evidence. We have only external rules of Christian prudence to enable us to judge by circumstances and to decide which is the more expedient. And we have not within us any certain rule to discern whether a decided preference for one right action over another is from a divine influence or from our own nature. And it would not suit our condition here to have this certainty; it is the will of God that we should remain in this uncertainty, and that we should not be able to distinguish between them. It is necessary, then, that this divine influence be adapted to our condition, and that it operate always without our consciousness.

The danger of illusion about venial acts is not astonishing when we are in a state in which we are liable to far more perilous errors that may lead us to mistake the motions of self-love, which are the death of the soul, for its true life. What will we do in this state of darkness? All that depends upon us to do. And with this we must be satisfied. Fidelity in duty, united to peaceful trust, in such a state of uncertainty, is the greatest self-sacrifice to those spirits who are eager to understand the ways of God.

It is true that, notwithstanding the obscurity that rests upon this pilgrimage, there are appearances that, although without absolute certainty, encourage in the heart a humble confidence that the Spirit of God guides it. There are gleams of this light in the darkness of the most uncertain faith, making it visible occasionally, so that we are led on to perfection by the divine love. God mingles light and darkness thus so that the soul may not be lost in uncertainty— yet also not have a full assurance and not find here, in either state, a sufficient support.

The best proof that we are influenced by the Spirit of God is, first, when the action itself is pure and conformable to the perfection of His laws. The second is when we perform it simply, tranquilly, without eagerness to do it, contented if it is necessary to relinquish it. The third is when, after the work is done, we do not seek by unquiet reflections to justify the action, even to ourselves, but are willing it should be condemned, or to condemn it ourselves, if any superior light discovers it to be wrong, and when we do not appropriate the action to ourselves but refer it to the will of God. The fourth is when this work leaves the soul in its simplicity, in its peace, in its own uprightness, in humility, and in self-forgetfulness.

All these things, it is true, are very delicate in their operation upon the mind, and all we can say still gives little knowledge of them. But though there is so much obscurity in a state of faith, it is nevertheless true that God, without teaching us by positive rules how to know His voice, accustoms the mind to understand it, to recognize it, and to obey it—although it cannot give an account by any philosophical principle or precise rule as to how it may be discerned. He gives to the soul, when it needs it, a momentary certainty, and then it is withdrawn, leaving no vestige behind. The greatest danger is in interrupting this influence by the restlessness with which we would escape from this state, and insisting upon seeing clearly when we are thus surrounded by darkness.

One thing that is desirable to observe is that we can often more easily distinguish the things that are from nature than the things that have a divine influence. Let us relinquish our own peculiar desires, whether they lead us to repose or to action—those that are induced by a refined intellectual taste, as entirely as those that grow out of the pleasures of sense—and in this peace of the soul, let us, in simplicity and truth, and in the presence of God, do all we can to die to ourselves and to please Him.

But we must guard against useless scruples, against a mental constraint and an anxiety to be assured that we perform all our actions under the influence of the Spirit of God. We may extinguish this light in the endeavor to ascertain that we are following it. We may return, under a pretext of safety, into all the windings of that self-love that we pretend to avoid. We are in danger of losing the reality of this influence in our effort to obtain a certainty with regard to it, which it is not the will of God that we should possess. Thus we might pass our lives in reasoning upon the operation of the Spirit of God without daring to yield ourselves up to its influence.

If I propose anything personal and peculiar to you, my good Duke, it would be to remind you that the bent of your mind and the temptation to illusion in you arise not from any gross disorders but from the intemperance of wisdom and the excess of reasoning. Even wisdom ought to be sober and temperate. Sobriety and simplicity of mind are the same thing. The practice of true love for God dissipates doubts and makes us despise speculative reasonings.

LETTER 5

To a Person in Affliction

It is, Madam, but a sad consolation to say to you that I feel your sorrow. This, however, is all that human weakness can do: and when we would do more, we must turn to God. It is to Him that I go, the consoler of the afflicted, the protector of the weak. I pray to Him, not that He may take away your grief from you, but that He may make it a blessing to you; that He may give you strength to support it, and that He may not let you sink under it. These great sorrows are the remedies for the diseases of our minds. It is through great suffering that the mystery of Christianity is accomplished—I mean the crucifixion of self. It is then that the grace of God is unfolded to us, that we understand its intimate operation upon us, and that we are taught to sacrifice self. We must turn our thoughts away from ourselves before we can give them to God; and so that we may be constrained to do this, it is necessary that our hearts be so deeply wounded that all created things are turned into bitterness to us. Thus touched in the tenderest part, troubled in its sweetest and purest affections, the heart feels that it cannot support itself, and it escapes from its weakness and goes to God.

These, Madam, are violent remedies, but sin has made them necessary. This is the true support of the Christian in affliction. God lays His hand upon two beings united in a holy affection. He confers a blessing upon both; He places one in glory and makes his removal the means of salvation to the one who remains. This is what God has done for you. May His Holy Spirit awaken all your faith so that you may penetrate these truths. I will pray for it continually, and as I have much faith in the prayers of the afflicted, I beg of you to remember me in your prayers. Your charity will teach you what I have need of and will give earnestness to your petitions.

LETTER 6

On the Death of a Pious Friend

God has taken what was His own. Has He not done right? It was time that F— rested from all his sufferings; they were great, and he thought little of them himself; his only inquiry was concerning the will of Him in whose hands he was. Crosses are of no use to us, except as we yield ourselves up to them and forget ourselves. Forget yourself, then, my friend; otherwise this sorrow will not be a blessing to you. God does not make us suffer for the sake of suffering but to teach us to forget ourselves in that state in which this self-forgetfulness is the most difficult—a state of great sorrow.

I feel for the grief of the good Abbé F—. I know how truly they were united, and I have been rejoiced at it. Such a death as this has nothing but joy in it. He is nearer to us than he was before. There is no longer any curtain between us. Even the veil of faith is raised to those whose hearts are full of a pure and disinterested love.

LETTER 7

To a Friend

Hearts united by religion meet, although separated by distance.

I am always united in heart to you and your dear family; never doubt it. We are near together, though we do not see each other; while many people are far apart, though they live in the same room. God unites all and annihilates distance to those whose hearts unite in Him. He is the common center, where hearts meet from all parts of the world. I cannot help feeling the privation of not seeing you. But we must submit to this with patience while it pleases God that it should be so, even if it should be till death. Content yourself with the performance of your own duties. For the rest, be composed and self-collected, diligent in regulating your own affairs, and patient under domestic trials.

As for Madam —, I pray God that she may not regard those things that are behind but press forward in the right path. I pray that God may bless all your family, and that they may belong to Him.

LETTER 8

On the Dangers of Mental Dissipation

No one could be more affected than I was by the excellent letter that you wrote me. I saw your heart in it, and I approve of it. I pray that God may preserve you amid the contagion of the age. Your security will be to distrust your quickness and natural activity. You have more than common taste for mental dissipation, and as soon as you are dissipated, you are weakened. As your strength can come only from God, you must not be astonished if you are weak as soon as you turn from Him. God supports us only when we trust in Him. Should He not allow us to fall when we rashly separate ourselves from Him? We can only hope for a resource against our weakness in meditation and prayer.

You are peculiarly in want of this support. You have an excitable disposition that is easily interested; your passions are soon awakened; your vivacity and your natural activity expose you. Besides, you have an open, frank manner that pleases and prejudices the world in your favor. Nothing is more dangerous than this power of pleasing. Self-love is delighted with it, and the heart is poisoned by it. At first, its victims are amused, then flattered, then dissipated; their good resolutions are weakened, and at last they are intoxicated with self and with the world, that is to say, with pleasure and vanity. Then they feel that they are separated from God, and they have no courage to return.

Your only security will lie in guarding yourself against this dissipation. I implore you to devote a quarter of an hour every morning to reading some religious book and to meditating upon it with freedom, simplicity, and affection. Employ a few moments more in the same way in the evening. And occasionally during the day, recall to your mind the presence of God and your intention of acting according to His will. Contemplate with humility your faults, and strive in earnest to correct them; be patient with yourself, without flattering your faults, just as you would be with another person. Observe the ordinances of your religion. I will pray with my whole heart for you.

LETTER 9

To a Person Living in Solitude

I will never forsake anyone whom God has committed to my care until I fail in my duty to God Himself; therefore, do not fear that I will forget you. But if I were to do so, God could effect by His immediate influence what His unworthy instrument had neglected. "Be not afraid, O you of little faith." Remain exactly in your usual state. Retain your confidence in N—, who knows the very bottom of your heart, and who alone can give you consolation in your trials. It will be given to him to aid you in your need. No convent will be suitable for you. Everything would be constraint to you and would prove a dangerous temptation. Remain free in solitude, and let your heart in simplicity be occupied with God and yourself. Every day is a feast day to those who endeavor to live only in the will of God. Place no limits to your devotion to Him. Never interrupt the operation of His Spirit.

There is a great difference between pain and trouble. Simple pain is a state of purification, while trouble is a state of punishment.

Pain, if we are not unfaithful, is sweet and tranquil because of the entire acquiescence of the soul in the will of God. But trouble is the rebellion of the heart against Him and an opposition of the will to itself; thus, the spirit is rent by the division. But pain only purifies the soul; to be willing to suffer is to be in peace. It is the blessed germ of Paradise in our state of probation. When we resist God, we lose the influence of His Spirit, and in losing this, we depart from peace and from that experience of Him that is to us what the pillar of fire by night and the cloud by day were to the Israelites in the desert.

LETTER 10

To a Married Woman

The day of Saint Francis de Sales is a great feast for me, Madam. You see by his letters and by his life that he had risen above the world. He received, with the same peace and the same self-for-getfulness, its greatest honors and its severest contradictions. His natural style discovers an amiable simplicity that is far above the charms of the spirit of this world. You see a man possessed of a profound penetration, exquisite judgment of things, and knowledge of the human heart, who sought only, as a simple man, to comfort, solace, enlighten, and perfect his neighbor. No one had a keener sense of the highest perfection, but he brings himself down to the meanest and lowest; he makes himself all things, not so that he may please, but so that he may gain all—not for himself but for Jesus Christ. This is the spirit of the saint that I wish to impart to you. To think of the world without either contempt or hatred—this is a life of faith. Be not intoxicated with its flatteries or discouraged by its contradictions, but maintain an equal mind between these two states, and walk in the presence of God with a peaceful constancy, looking—in the various appearances and actions of men—to God alone, who thus sometimes supports our weaknesses by consolations and sometimes kindly exercises our faith by trials. This is the true life of the children of God.

You will be happy if you can say from the very bottom of your heart, "Woe to the world." Its conversation and its pleasures have yet too much power over you. They do not deserve so much of your attention. The less you desire to please it, the more you will be above it. What is called *spirit* is only a vain refinement that the world teaches. There is no free spirit but simple and upright reason, and among the children of Adam there is no right reason if it is not purified and corrected by the Spirit of God, who can teach us all truth. (See John 16:13.)

If you wish to be directed by the Spirit of God, listen no longer to the world. Listen not to your own inclinations, for they are of the world. Desire no spirit but the spirit of the gospel, no refinements but those of the spirit of faith, which is conscious of the slightest imperfection in virtue. In seeking to be perfect in this way, with humility and simplicity, you will be compassionate toward the infirmities of others, and you will have a true refinement of mind, without disgust or contempt for things that appear low, mean, and in bad taste. Oh, how really low and vulgar is the refinement in which the world glories when compared to that which I desire for you with my whole heart.

LETTER 11

To the Same Person

Do not think, Madam, that I am wanting in zeal to do you good. I perceive your upright intentions and the thirst with which God has inspired you for all those truths that will prepare you for His service. I should rather die than be wanting in my duty to the souls who are confided to me, and more especially to yours, which is very dear to me in our Lord.

Your piety is too anxious and unquiet. Do not distrust God; if you are sincere, He will not fail you in your need. Either His providence will furnish you with assistance from without, or He will supply you with the power you want within yourself. Believe Him faithful in all His promises, and He will reward you according to the measure of your faith. Were you abandoned by all mankind in an inaccessible desert, He would send manna from heaven, and He would cause the water to flow from the rocks.

Fear only failing in your duty to Him, and do not fear even this so as to be troubled. Support yourself as you would support your neighbor, without flattering his faults. Be simple with him who dwells with the simple.

LETTER 12

To the Same Person

You are right in thinking that it is not enough to change the object of ardent feeling, and that there is an unquiet excitement that we should moderate even in the service of God and in the correction of our own defects.

This view should assist you in acquiring calmness without leading you to relax your efforts. The ardor with which you enter into the best things is an evil; it produces an agitation that becomes still more opposed to the peace of the Spirit of God, so that, from a sense of politeness, you are induced to control the expression of it. A little simplicity would enable you to practice the virtue with more success and less effort.

With regard to your apparel, it appears to me that you should be guided by the taste of your husband; it is for him to decide upon these little proprieties. If he wishes to practice economy in these things, you ought to retrench as far as may be agreeable to him. If he desires that you make a certain appearance, do out of complaisance to him whatever you think will please him, and yield to him your own taste and judgment.

If he does not regard these things and leaves you to yourself, a medium is the best. You are fond of extremes; entire magnificence alone can satisfy your refined and lofty taste. A severe simplicity is another refinement of self-love, for we then renounce grandeur in a striking manner. It is mediocrity that is insupportable to pride. There is the appearance of a lack of taste when you are dressed like a citizen. I am told that you once dressed like a nun. This was too much in appearance and too little in reality. A moderate appearance would cost you a greater sacrifice. You can be truly simple only by keeping a true medium. All extremes, even in right, have in them a refined affectation.

The mediocrity that excites no attention furnishes no aliment to self-love. It is the love of God only that does not suffer from these severe rules. Your plain duty is to speak without reserve to your husband and to do without hesitation whatever you see will please him.

LETTER 13

We Must Not Suffer from the Fear of the Death of Those Whom We Love

I partake of the grief that you feel at the dangerous illness of N—. The uncertainty that you have endured these two days past is a severe suffering. Nothing is a greater trial to human nature than this suspense between a weak hope and a great fear. But we must have faith in our grief. Our sensibility leads us to think that our afflictions will be greater than we can bear, but we do not know the strength of our own hearts or the power of God. He knows all. He knows every folding of the heart that is the work of His hand and the extent of the sorrow that He inflicts, and He will proportion the one to the other. Let Him do then His pleasure, and let us be willing to suffer. It is cowardice and sensitiveness that thinks something to be impossible which in truth is not. What we think will overwhelm us entirely only subdues and conquers our pride, which cannot be too much humbled. And the renewed spirit rises from its subjection with a celestial strength and celestial consolations. Commit your friend to God. What would be the sacrifice? The short and suffering life of a being who must endure pain on earth and who finds his safety in death. You will see him again soon, not under this sun that shines upon vanity and affliction of spirit, but in the pure light of eternal truth, which will make the felicity of all those who behold it.

The more pure and excellent your friend is, the more worthy he is of being set free from this world. It is true that there are few sincere friends, and that it is hard to lose them. But we do not lose them; the danger is only for ourselves, lest we should be lost in not following those whom we mourn.

As for your prayers, have no fears; there can be no illusion in encouraging the consciousness of the presence of God and letting your mind dwell upon His perfection.

While you think only of God, truly love Him and—remembering His presence—devote yourself to Him without presumption, and then, without neglecting any duty, you will be in no danger; follow then your inclinations.

LETTER 14

On the Difference between the Willingness to Suffer, which God Inspires, and the Courage of the Men of the World

I am touched with the sufferings of your sick friend, but I rejoice that he supports them so well. You are right in making a distinction between willingness to suffer and courage. Courage is a certain elevation and strength of mind with which people overcome everything. Those minds that are guided by the Spirit of God and that are conscious of their own weakness do what is necessary to be done without being aware of their own strength and without any assurance of success. They endure and overcome by an inexplicable power that is within them without their knowing it, which comes to them as occasion requires (as if it was borrowed), and which they do not think of appropriating to themselves. They are not thinking of suffering well, but, insensibly, they are able to bear every trial to the end, in peace and simplicity, without any other desire than that the will of God be fulfilled.

There is nothing brilliant, nothing grand, nothing striking in the eyes of others—and still less in their own eyes—in this. If you tell them that they have suffered nobly, they will not understand you. They do not know themselves how all this comes to pass; they scarcely know what is in their own hearts, and they do not seek to know. If they endeavored to know, they would lose something of their simplicity. This is what we call perfect good will, which makes less show but is far greater than what is called courage. It is like water; the less taste or color it has, the purer it is; and it is its purity that makes it transparent. This good will, which is only a love of the will of God, becomes, on every occasion, just what it should be, so that it may conform itself to Him. Happy are those who have the beginning, the seeds within them, of this unspeakable good!

LETTER 15

On Bearing with Ourselves with Charity and Endeavoring Quietly to Correct Our Faults

People who love themselves as they love their neighbor will endure their own failings—as they do their neighbor's—with charity. They will see the defects to be corrected in themselves as they see those of others, and they will manage themselves as they would another whom they would lead to God. They are patient with themselves and insist upon only those things that may be accomplished under present circumstances. They are not discouraged because they cannot be perfect in one day. They condemn, without any qualification, the slightest imperfection—they see it in all its deformity, they endure the consciousness of it in all humility and sorrow, and they neglect nothing to cure themselves—but they are not fretful in the performance of this duty. They do not listen to those murmurings of their pride and self-love, which would mingle their complaints with the deep yet quiet emotions that the Spirit of God inspires within us for the correction of our faults.

These useless murmurs only serve to discourage the soul, occupy it with all the refinements of self-love, separate it from God, lead it to seek for consolations contrary to His will, weary and distract and exhaust it, and prepare for it a sort of disgust and despair about being able to hold on its course.

Nothing retards the progress of the mind more than troubles of this nature, when we voluntarily seek them; but when we only endure them, without producing them by reflections induced by self-love, then they will, like our trials, become sources of virtue. They will be ranked among the other tests of our virtue, which God sees are necessary for our purification, and we must submit to them as we should to a fit of sickness.

Nevertheless, we must pursue our labor within and our outward acts of duty as far as we are at liberty to do it. Prayer will not be less a privilege in this state or less enjoyed. Our love will not be less animated and true. The presence of God will not be less distinct or less consoling, and our duties will not be less faithfully fulfilled. But our constancy is certainly greater when maintained under such painful circumstances. It is a greater force that carries a rowboat against wind and tide a quarter of a league than the one that impels it a whole league when it has them both in its favor.

We must treat this complaining of our self-love as some people treat the vapors. They take no notice of them and act as if they did not feel them.

LETTER 16

On Avoiding Anxiety about the Future and Living a Life of Faith and Trust in God

Do not dwell upon remote events; this anxiety about the future is contrary to a religious state of mind. When God bestows any blessing upon you, look only to Him in the comfort that you receive, and take every day of the manna that He sends you, as the Israelites did, without making yourself any provision for tomorrow.

A life of faith produces two things. First, it enables us to see God in everything. Second, it holds the mind in a state of readiness for whatever may be His will. We must trust in God for whatever depends upon Him, and only think of being faithful ourselves in the performance of our duties. This continual, unceasing dependence, this state of entire peace and acquiescence of the soul in whatever may happen, is the true, silent martyrdom of self. It is so slow and gradual and internal that those who experience it are hardly conscious of it.

When God deprives you of any blessing, He can replace it, either by other instruments or by Himself. The very stones can in His hands become the children of Abraham. Sufficient for the day is the evil thereof; tomorrow will take care of itself. (See Matthew 6:34.) He who has fed you today will take care of you tomorrow.

We will sooner see the manna fall from heaven in the desert than the children of God will lack support.

LETTER 17

On the Proper Contemplation of Our Defects

There is a very subtile illusion in your disquietude, for you appear to be occupied with what is due to God and His glory, but at the bottom, you are really full of yourself. You wish that God should be glorified, but it is by your own perfection; by this means, you enter into all the refinement and sinuosity of self-love. This is merely an ingenious contrivance for thinking of yourself. The true use to be made of all the imperfections of which you are conscious is neither to justify nor to condemn them but to present them before God, conforming your will to His and remaining in peace. For peace is the divine order, in whatever state we may be.

LETTER 18

True Friendship Is Found by Drawing Near to God and Subduing Self

We ought to receive, without any desire to choose for ourselves, whatever God gives us. It is right that His will and not ours should be done, and that, without any reserve, His will should become ours. Then this world would be like heaven. This is a far greater happiness than seeing and conversing with our friends or receiving the consolations they can afford.

How intimately we are united when we truly meet in the love and presence of God. How well we speak when our wills and our thoughts are full of Him who is all in all. Do you then desire true friends? Seek them only at the Source of eternal friendships. Do you wish to hold fellowship with them? Listen in silence to Him who is the word, the life, and the soul of all those who speak the truth and who live in uprightness. You will find in God not only all that you want but all that is so imperfectly manifested by those in whom you trust.

You cannot do too much to correct your natural impetuosity and habit of following your love of activity. To be silent, to suffer, to judge no one without actual necessity, and to listen to the voice of God within you—this will be like a continual prayer and sacrifice of self.

LETTER 19

On the Advantage of Being
Brought Near to Death

It is good for us to approach the gates of death. We become familiar with what we must very soon know. We ought to know ourselves better when we have come so near to the judgment of God and the rays of eternal truth. How great, how overwhelming, is the thought of God when we are so near to Him, when the veil that has hidden Him is so near to being lifted! Improve this grace of God toward you by detaching yourself from the world, and still more from yourself, for this clinging to others is in truth for the sake of self.

Love God, then, and renounce self in your love for Him. Love neither your spirit nor your courage. Cherish no self-complacency on account of the gifts of God to you, such as disinterestedness, equity sincerity, and generosity. All these are from Him, but they may be turned into poison if they inflate self-love. We must be little in our own eyes and ever act in this spirit.

LETTER 20

On Yielding What Is Due to Others and Still Devoting Time to Religious Meditation

I pity you, but we must suffer. We are placed in this world that we may be purified by sacrificing our own inclinations and dying to self. You are called upon for this sacrifice; do not shrink from it. I acknowledge that you should not relinquish your rules for the regulation of your time, but you may gain in detail what you lose in the mass. You must manage a little. You must proceed with caution and be guided by circumstances. Yield in little things; and in those that you think essential, you must exercise all your firmness. But remember that true firmness is gentle, humble, and tranquil. All violent, haughty, and unquiet firmness is unworthy of the cause of religion. When you are led to act with harshness, acknowledge it humbly but adhere to your principle and, while you confess the fault in your manners, maintain your rule.

With these restrictions, you cannot be too complaisant, too kind, or too affectionate. There is no book and no prayer that can improve you so much as this continual self-subjection, provided you make a proper use of it in your hours of retirement, and provided the dissipations of business do not exhaust the fountain of your affections. In summary, devote as much time as you can to religious meditation, and give the rest of your life to charity, which never faints, which suffers long, and which does not think of itself.

LETTER 21

On Calmly Enduring the Irregularities of Others

A heated imagination, violent feelings, hosts of reasons, and volleys of words effect nothing. The right way is to act as in the presence of God—divested of self, doing according to the light we have what we are able to do, and satisfied with what success He may grant us. This is a joyful state of self-oblivion that few persons understand. A word uttered in this simplicity and peace produces a greater effect, even in external affairs, than all the most violent and eager efforts. As it is the Spirit of God who speaks, He speaks with His power and authority; He enlightens, persuades, touches, and edifies. We seem to have said nothing, but we have done everything. On the contrary, when we are guided by our own natural impulses, we think we cannot say enough. We make a thousand vain and superfluous reflections. We are always afraid that we will not do or say enough. We are excited, we exhaust ourselves, we grow angry, we depart from the object, and no good is done.

Your temperament requires many of these lessons. Let the waters flow on in their course. Let men be men, that is to say, let them be vain, inconstant, unjust, false, and presumptuous. Let the world be the world; you cannot help it. Let each one follow his own bent and his own ways; you cannot form him over again. It is wiser to leave men to themselves and to endure them. Accustom yourself to unreasonableness and injustice. Remain at peace in the presence of God, who knows all your trials and permits them. Be satisfied with calmly doing all that depends upon you, and let the rest be as if it were not.

LETTER 22

On Suffering Ill-treatment with Humility and in Silence

I am touched, as I ought to be, with all your sorrows; but I can only pity you and pray God to console you. You greatly need His Spirit to support you in your trial and to temper your natural excitability on an occasion so calculated to awaken it. When God would teach us to die to ourselves, He touches us in the tenderest part; our weakness is the measure of our trial. Be humble. Silence and peace, in a state of humiliation, are the true health of the soul. We are tempted to speak humbly, and we find a thousand excuses for it; it is still better to be silent, for the humility that speaks may be suspected. Self-love consoles itself a little by speaking.

Do not be vexed at what people say. Let them speak while you endeavor to do the will of God. You will never succeed in pleasing men, and it would not be worth the trouble if you could. A little silence, peace, and communion with God will compensate you for all the injustice of men. We must love our fellow beings without depending upon their friendship. They leave us, they return, and they go from us again. Let them go or come; it is the feather blown about by the wind. Fix your attention upon God alone in your connection with them. He alone, through them, either consoles or afflicts you.

All your firmness is required in the situation in which you are placed, but your impetuosity must meet with trials and obstacles. Possess your soul in patience. Renew often within you the feeling of the presence of God so that you may learn moderation. There is nothing truly great except lowliness, charity, fear of ourselves, and detachment from the dominion of sense.

LETTER 23

On Carrying the Spirit of Prayer into All Our Actions

Do not be discouraged at your faults; bear with yourself in correcting them as you would with your neighbor. Lay aside this ardor of mind that exhausts your body and leads you to commit errors. Accustom yourself gradually to carry prayer into your daily occupations. Speak, move, and act in peace, as if you were in prayer. In truth, this is prayer.

Do everything without eagerness, as if by the Spirit of God. As soon as you perceive your natural impetuosity driving you, retire into the sanctuary where the Father of spirits dwells. Listen to what you there hear, and then do not say or do anything except what He dictates in your heart.

You will find that you will become more tranquil, that your words will be fewer and more to the purpose, and that with less effort you will accomplish more good. I do not recommend here a perpetual struggle of the understanding after something impracticable but a habit of quietness and peace in which you may take counsel of God with regard to duty. This you will find a simpler and shorter consultation than the eager and tumultuous debates that you usually hold with self when you yield to your natural impetuosity.

When the heart is fixed on God, it can easily accustom itself to suspending the natural movements of ardent feeling and to waiting for the favorable moment when the voice within may speak. This is the continual sacrifice of self and the life of faith. This death of self is a blessed life, for the grace that brings peace succeeds to the passions that produce trouble. Endeavour to acquire a habit of looking to this light within you; then all your life will gradually become a prayer. You may suffer, but you will find peace in suffering.

LETTER 24

On Our Duty in a State of Peace and Happiness

I rejoice that you are so pleased with your retreat and that God gives you so much peace within and without. I pray that the One who has commenced this good work will finish it. It is for you to profit by it. You must improve this time of peace by reflection. You must send up from your heart that continual Amen and that unceasing Hallelujah that resound through the heavenly Jerusalem. This is a perfect acquiescence in the will of God, and a sacrifice without any reserve of our will to His.

We must at the same time listen to the voice of God (with our hearts free from all flattering partialities of self-love), faithfully receive and attend to this light when it shows us our faults, and then correct them. What it points out as wrong, we must relinquish, however great be the sacrifice. When we thus yield ourselves up to the Spirit of God with a perfect renunciation of self, we discover imperfections in our best works, and find within us an inexhaustible fund of faults that were before imperceptible. Then we say that God alone is good. We strive to correct ourselves in a quiet and simple manner, but our efforts are continual, equal, efficacious, deep, and earnest to the extent that the heart is fixed and undivided.

While all our trust is in help from God, we do not relax our own exertions. We know that He will never fail us, and that it is only we who are unfaithful to Him. We condemn ourselves without being discouraged, and we correct our faults while we retain our strength.

LETTER 25

The Experience of Our Faults and the Difficulty of Curing Them Should Teach Us Humility

I acknowledge that I am glad to see you oppressed with a sense of your defects and your inability to correct them. This despair of nature that leads us to trust only in God is what He Himself wills. It is then that He gives us the aid we need.

It is true that you have a hasty and severe disposition and a fretful character that is too sensitive to the faults of others and that renders it difficult to efface impressions that you receive. But it is not your natural temperament that God condemns, for this you have not chosen and are not able to change. It may be the means of your salvation, if you bear it rightly as a trial. But what God requires of you is that you actually perform those duties for which His grace gives you ability. What is required is, if you cannot be gentle in your exterior, to be humble in your heart, to restrain your natural haughtiness as soon as you perceive it, and to repair the evil you have done, by your humility. The duty you are called to practice is a real, genuine lowliness of heart upon all occasions, a sincere renunciation of self.

It is not surprising that the high opinion entertained by many persons of your decisions for so many years has insensibly encouraged in you a secret confidence in yourself and a *hauteur* of which you are not aware.

The hasty expressions into which your temper sometimes betrays you may perhaps reveal to you the haughtiness that, without this natural frankness, you would not discover. But the source of the evil is within; it is this high opinion of yourself that has lain hidden so long under some specious name. Be then as humble in the contemplation of your own defects as you have been elevated by your office in judging the defects of others. Accustom yourself to seeing others neglect your opinion, and give up judging them. At least if you say anything, let it be said in simplicity, not to decide or correct but merely to propose a question and to seek information.

In a word, the object is to place yourself upon a level with the lowest and most imperfect and to encourage in them a freedom that must make it easy for them to open their hearts to you. If you have anything to bestow upon them, let it be consolation and support rather than correction.

LETTER 26

We Must Endure the Faults of Others and Be Willing Ourselves to Receive Blame

It appears to me that your heart wants enlargement with regard to the faults of others. I grant that you cannot help seeing them when they are presented to your notice, and you cannot avoid the opinions produced in your mind by the principles on which some people apparently proceed. You cannot even avoid a degree of pain that these things must occasion. It is enough if you are willing to bear with some faults, form no judgment in doubtful cases, and refuse to cherish that degree of pain that would separate you from those who are imperfect. Perfection easily supports the imperfections of others. It makes itself all things to all. We must familiarize ourselves with the greatest defects of good men and quietly leave them till the time when God will indicate the moment for undertaking their cure. Otherwise, we may destroy the good grain with the chaff.

Such persons must strive according to their strength for their own improvement, and we must bear with their weaknesses. You ought to remember from your own experience how bitter this correction is, and this should lead you to soften it for others. I ask of you, with more earnestness than ever, that you will not spare me with regard to my faults. If your opinion of my defects gives me pain, this sensibility will prove that you have touched me in the tender part. Thus you will have done me a great good in exercising my humility and accustoming me to blame. I ought to be more lowly in my mind as I am more elevated from my situation and as God demands of me a greater sacrifice of myself. I stand in need of this simplicity, and I hope it will strengthen the union between us.

LETTER 27

On the Circumspection that Is Necessary in Correcting Others and in Judging What Is Wrong

While we are so imperfect, we can understand only in part. The same self-love that causes our defects injuriously hides them from us and from others. Self-love cannot bear the view of itself. It finds some hiding place, and it places itself in some flattering light to soften its ugliness. Thus there is always some illusion in us, while we are so imperfect and have so much love of ourselves.

Self-love must be uprooted, and the love of God must take its place in our hearts, before we can see ourselves as we are. Then the same principle that enables us to see our imperfections will destroy them. When the light of truth has risen within us, then we see clearly what is there. Then we love ourselves without partiality and without flattery, as we love our neighbor. In the meantime, God spares us by uncovering our weakness to us, in proportion as our strength to support the view of our weakness increases. We discover our imperfections one by one as we are able to cure them. Without this merciful preparation that adapts our strength to the light within, we should be in despair.

Those who correct others ought to watch the moment when God touches their hearts; we must bear a fault with patience till we perceive His Spirit reproaching them within. We must imitate the One who gently reproves, so that they feel that it is less God than their own hearts who condemns them. When we blame with impatience because we are displeased with the fault, it is a human censure and not the disapprobation of God. It is a sensitive self-love that cannot forgive the self-love of others. The more self-love we have, the more severe are our censures. There is nothing so vexatious as the collision between one excessive self-love and another still more violent and sensitive. The passions of others are infinitely ridiculous to those who are under the dominion of their own. The ways of God are very different. He is ever full of kindness for us. He gives us strength, He regards us with pity and condescension, He remembers our weakness, and He waits for us. The less we love ourselves, the more considerate we are of others. We wait even years to give salutary advice. We wait for Providence to give the occasion and the grace to open their hearts to receive it. If you would gather the fruit before its time, you lose it entirely.

Our imperfect friends can know us only imperfectly; the same self-love that hides their defects magnifies ours. They see in us what we cannot see, and they are unacquainted with what we ourselves know. They are quick to identify what is disagreeable to them, but they do not perceive the defects that lie deep within and that sully our virtues and displease God alone. Thus, their best judgments are superficial.

My conclusion is that we must listen to the voice of God in the silence of our souls, and pronounce for or against ourselves whatever this pure light may reveal to us at the moment when we endeavor to know ourselves. We must often silently listen to this Teacher within, who will make known all truth to us, and who, if we are faithful in attending to Him, will often lead us to silence. When we hear this secret, small voice within, which is the soul of our soul, it is a proof that self is silent so that it may listen to Him. This voice is not a stranger there. God is in our souls as our souls are in our bodies. It is something that we cannot distinguish exactly, but it is what upholds and guides us. This is not a miraculous inspiration, which exposes us to illusion and fanaticism. It is only a profound peace of the soul that yields itself up to the Spirit of God, believing His revealed Word and practicing His commands as dared in the gospel.

LETTER 28

A Letter of Consolation

I think much of you and your sufferings. God will send His consolations into the depths of your soul. The wound is terrible, but His hand is all-powerful to heal. It is only the senses and the imagination that have lost their object. The one we do not see is more truly with us than he ever was. We will meet him in our common center. Although I have not seen him for many years, yet I have felt as if I conversed with him. I have opened my heart to him and believed that we have met in the presence of God; and although I have wept bitterly at his death, I cannot think that I have lost him. Oh, the reality of this intimate and invisible communion that the children of God enjoy!

I am anxious about your health; when the heart is sick, the whole body suffers. I fear that every object may awaken your grief. We must enter into the designs of God and try to receive the comforts that He bestows. We will soon find him whom we seem to have lost; we approach him with rapid strides. Yet a little while, and we will shed no more tears. We will die ourselves. The one we love lives and will never die. This is what we believe; if we believe it rightly, we will feel, in respect to our friends, as Jesus Christ wished that His disciples should feel toward Him when He rose to heaven. *"If ye loved me,"* said He, *"ye would rejoice* [in My glory]" (John 14:28). But we weep for ourselves. For a true friend of God who has been faithful and humble, we can only rejoice at his happiness and at the blessing that he has left upon those who belonged to him on earth. Let your grief, then, be soothed by the hand of Him who has afflicted you.

LETTER 29

On the Effects of Effeminacy and Rules of Conduct by which It May Be Overcome

Your greatest danger is from effeminacy and love of pleasure. These two defects may put the soul in dreadful disorder, even where it has resolved to practice virtue and feels a great horror of vice. Effeminacy is a languor of the mind that paralyzes and destroys its better life; it hides within it a treacherous flame that evil passions are ever ready to kindle and that will consume all before it.

We must cherish, then, a manly, vigorous faith that, without even listening to this weakness, can conquer it. As soon as we listen to it or make any terms with it, we are lost. It injures us as much in our connection with the world as with God. An effeminate man devoted to amusements will ever be a poor man, and if he ever gets into an important place, he will dishonor it. A love of ease will lead him away from his true interest. He cannot cultivate his talents, acquire the knowledge necessary for his profession, submit to the labor of a difficult office, endure the constraint that is necessary to please others, or apply himself courageously to the correction of his faults.

What will such a man do? He is good for nothing; he is incapable of any good thing, but he may fall into great evils. Pleasure will betray him. It is not for nothing that the senses are flattered. After appearing indolent and insensible, they will become furious and ungovernable, and this consuming fire will not be perceived till it can no longer be quelled.

Even your religious sentiments, if they are mingled with this effeminate spirit, while they may lead you to a life of seriousness and exterior decency, will have nothing real in them. You think much of relinquishing the follies of youth; religion is only a pretext for abandoning them. The truth is that they are irksome to you. You have lost your relish for them, and it is a matter of taste with you to lead a serious and sober life. But this seriousness, I fear, is as vacant and as dangerous as the folly and gaiety of pleasure. A serious sensualist, whose passions reign amid gloom and retirement, leads an obscure, cowardly, and corrupt life, at which the world, earthly-minded as it is, shudders with horror. You may quit the world, not for God, but to be devoted to your passions, or at least for a life of indolence that is offensive to God and that, in the eyes of men, is more contemptible than the most depraved passions. You may relinquish great objects in order to be absorbed with toys and amusements so trifling that any but children should blush to regard them.

Again, I repeat to you what I said at first. Effeminacy enervates and contaminates all who yield to it. It takes its strength and marrow from every virtue and from every power of the soul, even in the opinion of the world. Its victims are weak and inefficient in everything. God rejects them, and the world spurns them. Such a man is a nonentity; he is as if he were not.

He is not a man. Fear this defect that will be the source of so many others. Pray and watch. Watch against yourself. Rouse yourself as you would rouse a man in a lethargy. Make your friends stimulate you and awaken you from sleep. Have recourse to the ordinances of religion. Do not forget that, in this instance, the rewards of the world and of heaven are to be won in the same way. Both of these kingdoms are to be taken by violence. (See Matthew 11:12.)

LETTER 30

Advice relative to External Conduct and to the Management of Our Minds

I am not astonished at the disgust you feel at seeing so much that is opposed to the will of God; it is the natural effect of your change of heart. You now enjoy a certain calm in which you may be entirely occupied with what is so interesting to you, and be freed from all that would again open the wounds of your heart. But this is not the will of God. Bear this cross, then, in peace, as an expiation of your offenses, and wait till He liberates you from it. He will do it in His own time, not in yours.

In the meantime, set apart certain hours to think of God and your relation to Him. You must read, pray, distrust your inclinations and habits, remember that you carry the gift of God in an earthen vessel, and, above all, let your soul be nourished with the love of God. However you may have departed from Him, do not fear to return to Him with a humble and childlike love. Speak to

Him in your prayers of all your wretchedness, of all your wants, of all your sufferings. Speak even of the disrelish you sometimes feel for His service. You cannot speak too freely or with too much confidence. He loves the simple and the lowly; it is with them that He converses. If you are of this number, open your whole heart and say all to Him. After you have thus spoken to God, be silent and listen to Him. Let your heart be in such a state of preparation that His Spirit may impress upon you such virtues as will please Him. Let all within you listen to Him. This silence of all outward and earthly affections and of human thoughts within us is essential if we want to hear this voice that calls upon us to deny ourselves and to worship God in spirit and in truth. (See John 4:23–24.)

You have great helps in the knowledge you have acquired; you have read many good books; you are acquainted with the true foundations of religion and with the weakness of all that is opposed to it. But all these means, which might conduct you to God, will finally arrest your progress if you value too highly your own wisdom. –

The best and highest use of your mind is to learn to distrust yourself, to renounce your own will, and to submit to the will of God in order to become as a little child. It is not of doing difficult things that I speak but of performing the most common actions with your heart fixed on God and as one who is accomplishing the end of his being. You will act as others do, except that you will never sin. You will be a faithful friend—polite, attentive, complaisant, and cheerful—at those times when it is becoming in a true Christian to be so. You will be moderate at table, moderate in speaking, moderate in expense, moderate in judging, moderate in your diversions, and temperate even in your wisdom and foresight. It is this universal sobriety in the use of the best things that is taught us by the true love of God. We are not austere, fretful, or scrupulous, but we have within ourselves a principle of love that enlarges the heart and sheds a gentle influence upon everything, that, without constraint or effort, inspires a delicate apprehension (lest we should displease God), and that arrests us if we are tempted to do wrong.

In this state we suffer, as other people do, from fatigue, embarrassments, misfortunes, bodily infirmities, trials from ourselves, trials from others, temptations, disgusts, and sometimes discouragements. But if our crosses are the same with those of the rest of the world, our motives for supporting them are very different. We have learned from Jesus Christ how to endure. This can purify; this can detach us from self and renew the spirit of our minds. We see God in everything, but we have the clearest vision of Him in suffering and humiliation.

Live, my friend, without any exterior change but what may be necessary, either that you may avoid evil, may be protected against your weakness, or may not discredit the gospel. Beyond this, do not let your left hand know what your right hand does (see Matthew 6:3); endeavor to be cheerful and tranquil.

Regulate your expenses and your business. Be honorable and modest, simple and free. Serve your country from duty, not from ambition or vain hopes. This will be serving your country, your king, and the King of Kings, before whom all visible glories are but shadows.

Let your conduct be single, moderate, and without affectation of either good or evil, but be really firm in the cause of virtue and so decided that no one can hope to lead you astray. When it is evident that you are devoted in good faith to the cause of religion, no one will make the attempt to turn you from your course.

Do not put your trust in your resolutions or your own strength but in the goodness of God, who has loved you when you thought not of Him and before you could love Him.

LETTER 31

Consolation upon the Death of a Son

Your grief is present to me. I cannot forget the great loss you have met with; but God has taken what was His own and not ours. Who will say to Him, "What do You do?" You are far from saying it. His good pleasure is the supreme reason. Besides, amid the most severe sorrows, we can see His paternal hand and a secret design of mercy.

In another life, we will see and understand the wonders of His goodness that have escaped us in this, and we will rejoice at what has made us weep on earth. Alas, in our present darkness, we cannot see either our true good or evil. If God were to gratify our desires, it would be our ruin. He saves us by breaking the ties that bind us to earth. We complain because God loves us better than we know how to love ourselves. We weep because He has taken those whom we love away from temptation and sin. We would possess all that delights and flatters our self-love, though it might lead us to forget that we are exiles in a strange land. God takes the poisonous cup from our hands, and we weep as a child weeps when his mother takes away the shining weapon with which he would pierce his own breast.

Your son succeeded in the world; it is this success that makes you weep, but it was this that, in the counsels of the Almighty, perhaps, was the cause of his removal—in mercy both to him and to his friends. We must be silent and adore. Prayer alone can console you; it is only in prayer that we are truly in the presence of God.

As soon as we are with God in faith and in love, we are in prayer. And the most holy occupation that does not bring us in this way into His presence may be a study, but is not prayer. God is our only consoler. Remain in silence in His presence; He will comfort you. We will find all that we have lost in Him. Happy are those who desire no other consolation. This is pure and inexhaustible.

LETTER 32

On the Necessity of Joining
Freedom to Exactness

It appears to me that great freedom and great exactness should be united. Exactness makes us faithful, and freedom makes us courageous. If you are very strict without being free, you will become servile and scrupulous. If you are free without being strict, you will become negligent and careless. Those who have little experience of the ways of God think they cannot unite these two virtues. They understand *being exact* to mean living in constraint, sorrow, and a timid and scrupulous unquietness that destroys the repose of the soul, that finds sin in everything and is so narrow-minded that it questions about the merest trifles and dares hardly to breathe. They define *being free* as having an easy conscience, not regarding small things, being contented with avoiding great faults, not considering any but gross crimes as faults, and (with the exception of these) allowing whatever flatters self-love, and any license to the passions, that does not produce what they call "great evil."

It was not thus that Saint Paul understood things when he said to those whom he endeavored to make Christians, "Be free, but with the liberty that Jesus Christ has given you. Be free, for the Savior has called you to liberty, but let not this liberty be an occasion or pretext for evil." (See, for example, Galatians 5:13.)

It appears to me that true fidelity consists in obeying God in everything, following the light that points out our duty, and His Spirit, who prompts us to do it, having the desire to please Him, without debating about great or little sins or about imperfections or unfaithfulness. For though there may be a difference in fact, to the soul that is determined to do *all* His will, there is none. It is in this sense that the apostle says, "The law is not for the upright; the law constrains, menaces, if I may so speak, tyrannizes over us, enslaves us. But there is a superior law that raises us above all this and introduces us into the true liberty of the children of God." (See 1 Timothy 1:9.) It is this: that we ever desire to do all that we can to please our Father in heaven. According to the excellent instruction of Saint Augustine, "Love God and then do all you wish."

To this sincere desire to do the will of God, we must add a cheerful spirit that is not overcome when it has failed but begins again and again to do better, hoping always to the very end to be able to do it, bearing with its own involuntary weakness as God bears with it, waiting with patience for the moment when it will be delivered from it, going straight on in singleness of heart according to the strength that it can command, and losing no time by looking back or making useless reflections upon its falls, which can only embarrass and retard its progress. The first sight of our little failures should humble us, but then we must press on, not judging ourselves with a Judaical rigor and not regarding God as a spy who is watching for our least offense, or as an enemy who places snares in our path, but as a Father who loves and wishes to save us. We must trust in His goodness, invoke His blessing, and doubt all other support; this is true liberty.

I advise you to aspire after it. Fidelity and freedom should go hand in hand, but I fear with you that there is more danger of your desire for confidence in God and openness of heart to Him. I do not hesitate to advise you to yield yourself up entirely to that grace with which He calls you to Himself.

LETTER 33

On Submission to Occasional Indifference and Disrelish for Religion

I am not astonished at this lukewarmness in you. We cannot always be in raptures. It is good for us, by these occasional inequalities, to learn that it is a gift of God. If we were always in rapture, we should be insensible to suffering and to our own weakness; temptations would no longer be real temptations to us. We must be tried by this rebellion of our hearts so that our love of God may be purified. We are never more faithful than when we cling to our Creator, not by the joy of our hearts but in the entire choice and acquiescence of our wills. Outward sufferings would not be really painful if we were exempt from those within.

Submit to your indifference, then, with patience; it will be more useful to you than enjoyment that is accompanied with confidence in yourself. This trial, provided your will is faithful, is useful; it may be a great good to you. It may teach you humility and distrust of yourself. It may, by making you conscious of your weakness, lead you to put your whole trust in God. This sensible pleasure that you desire is neither the love of God nor the spirit of prayer.

Enjoy this pleasure when God bestows it, and when He does not grant it, still love Him and pray to Him as if you felt it. If God would prove you by the privation of this immediate pleasure in religion, you must enter into His designs of mercy toward you, and humbly submit to it. It will serve to destroy your self-love, and this is the will of God.

Your sufferings spring altogether from yourself; they are your own creation. It is a sensitiveness of self-love that you cherish in the bottom of your heart. Instead of performing your duties, helping others to support their burdens, and consoling those whom God has committed to your charge, you are ever recurring to self and thinking of your own discouragements.

Hope in God; He will support you and enable you to be useful to others if you trust in Him and do not neglect your duty.

LETTER 34

On Turning the Experience of Our Own Weakness to Advantage

I was quite grieved yesterday to see your mind so much disordered. It appears to me that there are two things you ought to do. One is never to voluntarily yield to your self-love; the other is never to be discouraged at discovering in your heart these unreasonable discontents. Would you do well? Ask God to make you patient with others and with yourself.

If you had only the defects of others to bear with, if you found weakness only in them, you would be strongly tempted to think yourself superior to your neighbor. God compels you, by a continual experience of your own defects, to acknowledge how just it is that you should bear with gentleness the faults of others.

Turn these weaknesses to your advantage by submitting to them, ingenuously confessing them, and accustoming yourself not to depend upon your own strength. The Spirit of God will aid you in the correction of your faults. Be patient with yourself, be humble, and resign yourself to your own imperfections, not neglecting to cure them but drawing from them a lesson of self-distrust, as we draw the most powerful remedies even from poisons. God makes you feel your weaknesses so that you may put your trust in Him. He will gradually deliver you from them. Happy indeed will be this deliverance!

LETTER 35

On the Causes of True Discretion and the Contrary Defect

With regard to discretion, I do not wish you to labor to acquire it by continual efforts and reflections upon your own conduct; this would produce too much constraint. It is better to be silent and find discretion in simplicity. We ought not, however, to be so silent as to be deficient in frankness and complaisance in our moments of relaxation and amusement; but then we may speak of indifferent things and suppress whatever may do harm.

In our recreations, we ought to have a sort of joyousness that will induce us to please others and be pleased with trifles. You will become prudent when you yield yourself to the Spirit of God. He is the Source of true prudence; ours gives us only a false dignity, a dazzling appearance, a factitious power. When we are truly simple and humble and stripped of our own wisdom, we are clothed with that of God, which cannot do wrong.

It is not the childlike simplicity of the Christian that produces our daily indiscretions; on the contrary, we commit more faults because we are thinking so much of our own wisdom and are afraid to give ourselves up to the guidance of the Spirit of God. This Spirit would lead us to speak or be silent, according to the call of the moment, without making any unquiet reflections upon ourselves or having that great desire to succeed that spoils the best things.

LETTER 36

On the Artifices of a Refined Self-love

I commit you to God, and I wish that you would commit yourself to Him. You hope for repose elsewhere than in God. You shut your heart to Him, and you try to repulse His merciful hand. Who has resisted God and been at peace? (See Job 9:4.) Return to Him, give yourself up to Him, and hasten to Him. Every moment of delay is a new infidelity. My heart is stricken for you; I hoped to find real consolation in you.

Oh, my dear daughter, be subdued by His Spirit. Allow me to place before you what seems to me to be His will for me to present to your view. From your earliest infancy you have unconsciously cherished in your heart an immoderate self-love under the disguise of delicacy, and a taste for romance, of which no one has shown you the illusion. You display it in the world, and you manifest it in your most pious actions.

I perceive in you always an alarming taste for what you call *esprit*, for what you think is graceful, and for little refinements.

This habit will make you find annoyances in every situation. With a mind really upright and powerful, this will render you inferior to many who have less of a mind than yourself. You give good advice to others, but you are overcome by the most extreme trifle yourself. Everything troubles you. You are in continual fear of committing a fault, or you are vexed that you have been guilty of one. You magnify faults by your lively imagination, and there is always some nothing that reduces you to despair. In one person you see nothing but defects, while in another you imagine perfections of which he has not even the shadow. Your refinement and generosity on one side, and your jealousies and distrusts on the other, are without measure or reason.

You are willing to give yourself up to others, but this makes you an idol to yourself and to them. Here is the origin of this refined idolatry of self that God wants to overthrow in your heart. The operation is violent but necessary. Go to the end of the world for consolation to your self-love, and you will find only that the disease increases. You must either offer it up as a sacrifice to God or be continually supplying it with new aliment. If you had no one to minister to your self-love, you would seek, under some pretext or other, for someone who would, and you would at last descend to the meanest and vilest subjects to gratify its cravings. There is only one remedy for you, and it is the very one from which you fly. The sufferings that you complain of spring from yourself. You repulse the hand of God; you listen only to your self-love; you bear this venom in your heart. Go where you will, you cannot escape God's displeasure.

Yield yourself up to Him, and learn to see yourself as you are—vain and ambitious of the admiration of others, seeking to become their idol to gratify your own idolatry of self, jealous and suspicious beyond measure, and fast sinking into an abyss. You must make yourself familiar with these dreadful thoughts; it is only in this way that you can dissolve the charm that enslaves you. You may drive away thought for a time, and you may cherish a vain and deceitful strength, such as a fever gives to a sick man, but it is still delirium.

There is no peace except in the destruction of our self-love. You may make some convulsive movements of strength and gaiety, but it is agony that prompts them. If you would make the same effort for the peace of God as you make against it, how unspeakable would be your happiness. I will pray God to give you strength to subdue yourself. I will pray Him to take pity upon your weakness and to do you good in spite of your resistance to Him. For myself, I will not forsake you.

LETTER 37

We Must Not Be Discouraged at the Imperfections of Our Fellow Creatures

I am very sorry for the imperfections you find in human beings, but we must learn to expect little from them; this is the only security against disappointment. We must receive from them what they are able to give us, as from trees the fruits that they yield. God bears with imperfect beings, even when they resist His goodness. We ought to imitate this merciful patience and endurance. It is only imperfection that complains of what is imperfect. The more perfect we are, the more gentle and quiet we become toward the defects of others.

Do not attend to those who, under the dominion of prejudice, erect themselves into a tribunal of justice. If anything can cure them, it is to leave them to themselves and to go on in your own path with the simplicity and meekness of a child.

LETTER 38

Our Efforts for Ourselves Should Be Within and Not in Externals

You are virtuous. You wish to be still more so, and you expend much effort on the details. But I fear you attend a little too much to externals. Think less of outward things and more of those within. Be willing to sacrifice to God the most powerful affections—your natural haughtiness, your worldly wisdom, your taste for show in your house, your fear of losing the consideration of the world, and your severity against what is irregular.

Your temper is what I am least concerned about. You are aware of it, and you fear it. Notwithstanding your resolutions, it overcomes you, and this teaches you humility and will help you to correct more dangerous faults.

Place your greatest dependence upon prayer; mere human strength and attention to precise forms will never cure you. But accustom yourself, from a consideration of your own incurable weaknesses, to view those of others with charity and compassion. Prayer will soften your heart and render you gentle, docile, accessible, and accommodating. Could you bear that God should be as strict with you as you are with your neighbor?

We are very severe about externals and do not look within. While we are scrupulous about a superficial display of virtue, we do not regard the coldness of our secret hearts toward God. We fear Him more than we love Him. We would pay our duty to Him with actions, and think we have settled our account with Him, instead of giving Him, without any calculation, all our love. If we looked carefully into ourselves, we should find some secret place where we hide what we think we are not obliged to sacrifice to God. We try not to see it, lest we should reproach ourselves for retaining it. We guard it as we would the apple of the eye. If anyone should force this entrenchment, he would touch us to the quick, and we should be inexhaustible in reasons to justify our attachment. The more we dread to renounce it, the more reason there is for believing that this is our duty. Our thoughts hover around ourselves, and we cannot forget ourselves in God. Why is it that the vessel does not sail? Is it that there is no wind? No, the breath of heaven never fails, but the vessel is held fast by anchors that we do not perceive; they are at the bottom of the deep.

The fault is our own and not our Creator's. We have only to seek for them, and we will find these hidden chains that bind us and arrest our progress. And there, where we least suspect, is the place where we should feel the most distrust.

Let us make no bargain with God, as if we feared our service to Him should cost us too much. Do not let us be satisfied with prayer, morning and evening, but let the whole day be one continual prayer.

LETTER 39

On the Death of the Abbé de Langeron, His Earliest and Most Faithful Friend

I have not the strength that you impute to me; I have felt my irreparable loss with a despondency that proves that my heart is very weak. Now I am calmer, and all that remains is a sort of bitterness and languor of soul. But this humbles me as much as my more violent grief. All that I have felt in both these states was self-love. I acknowledge that I have wept for myself in mourning for a friend who made the delight of my life and whose loss I feel continually. I find alleviation in the lassitude of grief, and my imagination, which was excited by a blow so unexpected, has become accustomed to the thought and is now calm.

But alas, everything is vain except an entire yielding up of our hearts to the Spirit of God. As for our friend, his death was so calm and peaceful that it would have made you happy to witness it. Even when he was delirious, his thoughts were all of God.

I never witnessed anything more edifying or lovely. I relate this to you because I ought not to speak of my great suffering without also acknowledging this joy of faith of which Saint Augustine speaks, and which God has granted me upon this occasion. He has done His will; He has preferred the happiness of my friend to my comfort. I should be wanting in my love for God and for my friend if I did not acquiesce in His will.

In my deepest grief, I have offered him, whom I so dreaded to lose, to God. I cannot help being touched at the tenderness with which you feel for me. I pray that the One whose love inspires you may reward you a hundredfold.

LETTER 40

To the Duke of Burgundy: That the Love of God Ought to Be Our Principle of Action, Our End, and Our Rule in Everything

The true way to love our neighbor is found in the love of God. We must love other beings in Him and for Him. Mankind does not understand the love of God; therefore, they fear it and separate themselves from it. It is because of this fear that they cannot realize this filial and intimate communion of children with a beneficent parent. They think only of a powerful and severe master. They are ever constrained and troubled in their interactions with God. They perform good actions with unwillingness, that they may avoid punishment; they would do evil if they dared, if they could hope to do it with impunity.

The love of God is an oppressive debt that they think they must pay; they try to elude it by the performance of certain ceremonies and an external homage, which they would substitute for a sincere and practical love of God. They practice arts with their Creator and hope to escape by giving the least they possibly can to Him. Oh, if men did but know what the love of God is, they would not desire any other felicity.

The love of God demands of us only innocent and right conduct. It bids us do for His sake what reason dictates to be done. It calls upon us to do from love for Him what men of the world do from a sense of honor or from self-love. It forbids nothing that the right exercise of reason does not forbid. Let us place everything in the order in which God has established it in the world. Let us do the same right things, but let us do them for the sake of Him who created us and to whom we owe everything.

This love of God does not demand of Christians those austerities practiced by hermits. It seldom requires brilliant and heroic actions or the renunciation of any rightful possessions; it only commands us not to make them our idols but to enjoy them in the divine order and with our hearts fixed on the Giver. The love of God does not increase the number of our trials; we find these already thickly scattered over every condition of life. They spring from the infirmities of our bodies and from our passions; they arise from our imperfections and from those of others with whom we are obliged to live. It is not the love of God that causes these sufferings; on the contrary, it is this alone that can soften them by the consolations it yields. It diminishes them, for it moderates our ardent passions and unreasonable sensibilities, which are the causes of all our real evils. If the love of God were genuine in our hearts, it would cure our griefs and fill us with a peaceful joy.

People are great enemies to themselves in resisting and fearing this pure sentiment. It renders all other precepts light and easy. What we do from fear is always wearisome, hard, painful, and oppressive. But all that we do from love, from persuasion, from a free and willing mind, however it may oppose the pleasures of sense, becomes agreeable to us. The desire of pleasing God makes us willing to suffer, if it is His will that we should. The sorrow in which we acquiesce is no longer a sorrow.

The love of God never disturbs the order of things that He has established. It leaves the great in their grandeur and makes them little only in His sight who has made them great. It leaves those whose condition is low in their lowliness and makes them contented with being nothing, except in His sight. This willingness to be in the lowest place has nothing of debasement in it; it is true greatness.

The true love of God regulates and inspires all our attachments. We never love our neighbor so truly as when our love for him is prompted by the love of God. All other foundations for our affections have reference to self. It is ourselves whom we love in our friends, and this is an imperfect love. It is more like self-love than real friendship.

How, then, must we love our friends? We must love them in the way that God has ordained. We must love God in them. We must love the good things with which God has endowed them, and we must, for His sake, submit to the privation of those things that He has denied them. When we love them with reference to self, our self-love makes us impatient, sensitive, and jealous, demanding much and deserving little, ever distrusting ourselves and our friends. It soon becomes wearied and disgusted; it very soon sees the termination of what it believed was inexhaustible. It meets everywhere with disappointment; it looks for what is perfect and finds it nowhere. It becomes dissatisfied, changes, and has no repose; while the friendship that is regulated by the love of God is patient with defects and does not insist upon finding in our friends what God has not placed there. It thinks of God and of what He has given; it thinks that all is good, provided it is from Him, and it can support that which God allows and that which He wills us to submit to by conforming ourselves to His designs.

The love of God never looks for perfection in created beings. It knows that it dwells with Him alone. As it never expects perfection, it is never disappointed. It loves God and all His gifts to every living thing, according to their respective value. It loves less what is less excellent and more what is nearer to perfection. It loves all, for there is no one who is not endowed with some good thing that is the gift of God, and it remembers that the vilest may become good and receive that grace which they now lack.

The one who loves God loves all His works—all that He has commanded us to love. He loves more those whom God has pleased to render dearer to Him. He sees in an earthly parent the love of his heavenly Father. In a relative, in a friend, he acknowledges those tender ties that God has ordained. The more strictly these bonds are in the order of His providence, the more the love of God sanctions them and renders them strong and intimate.

Can we love God without loving those whom He has commanded us to love? It is He who inspires this love; it is His will that we should love them. Will we not obey Him? This love can endure all things, suffer all things, and hope all things for our neighbor. It can conquer all difficulties; it flows from the heart and sheds a charm upon the manners. It is melted at the sorrows of others and thinks nothing of its own. It gives consolation where it is needed. It is gentle and adapts itself to others. It weeps with those who weep and rejoices with those who rejoice. It is all things to all men, not in a forced appearance and in cold demonstrations, but from a full and overflowing heart, in which the love of God is a living spring of the tenderest, the deepest, and the truest feeling. Nothing is so sterile, so cold, or so senseless as a heart that loves only itself in all things; while nothing can exceed the frankness, the tenderness, the gentle loveliness of a heart filled and animated by the divine love.

From "The Letters on Religion"

LETTER 41

The Soul of Man Is Immortal

This question is not a difficult one when it is reduced to its just limits. It is true that the soul of man is not a being by itself, possessing a necessary existence. There is but One who derives His existence solely from Himself, and who can never lose it, and who imparts it to others according to His pleasure.

God need not exercise a direct power to annihilate the soul of man. He would only have to withdraw that which has sustained his being every moment from his birth in order to re-plunge him into the nothingness from whence He originally drew him—as a man would merely open his hand to let a stone fall that he had held in the air.

The question that may reasonably be asked is not whether the soul of man may be annihilated, if it were the will of God; it is manifest that it might be. But the inquiry is, what is His will with regard to it?

Does, then, the soul contain within itself the seeds of destruction, which must, after a time, terminate its existence? Or, can we prove, philosophically, that it does not? The following is a negative proof.

When we think of the essential distinctions between the body and the soul, we are astonished at their union; and it is only by the operation of the power of God that we can comprehend how they can be so united and made to act in concert, though composed of such different elements. The body does not think. The soul is indivisible, has no extent or form, and is invested with none of the properties of the body. Ask anyone if his thoughts are round or square, white or yellow, cold or hot, divisible into six or twelve pieces—and instead of answering you, he will laugh at the question. Ask him if the atoms of which his body is composed are wise or foolish; if they know themselves, if they are virtuous; whether the round atoms have more sense and goodness than the square—and he would still only laugh and could hardly believe you were in earnest.

Go a little farther and imagine the atoms of whatever form you please—make them as impalpable as possible—and ask if it can be that a moment will come when these atoms, from being without any consciousness, will begin all at once to know themselves, to understand all that is around them, and to say to themselves, "I believe this, and I do not believe that"; "I love this thing, and I hate another." The person of whom you would ask these questions would call it child's play.

The absurdity of these questions proves that none of the ideas that we have of the nature of bodies enters into our conceptions of mind; that we do not connect the thinking being with the body or the being of space. As the distinction is so radical, the natures of these two beings so opposed, it is not astonishing that their union should be dissolved without either of them ceasing to exist. We ought, on the contrary, to be surprised that two natures so unlike can continue their operations in harmony for so long a time. What, then, should we conclude? That one of these beings will be annihilated as soon as its unnatural union with the other will cease? Imagine two bodies of exactly the same nature; separate them, and you destroy neither. As the one is not the other, it may exist or be annihilated without reference to the other. Their separation produces their mutual independence. But if we may reason thus of two bodies, really of the same nature, with how much more reason may we use this argument in relation to the soul and the body, whose union seems unnatural since they are so unlike in everything? On the other hand, the cessation of this transient union of these two natures cannot be to either the cause of its destruction. The annihilation of one would not be, on any ground, the cause of the annihilation of the other. A being that has not been the cause of the existence of another cannot be the cause of its annihilation. It then is clear as day that the disunion of the body from the soul cannot cause the annihilation of either, and that even the destruction of the body cannot put an end to the existence of the soul.

The union of the body and the soul consists only in a mutual concert or relationship between the thoughts of the one and the movements of the other; it is easy to see what the cessation of their connection would produce. It is a forced union between two beings entirely dissimilar and independent. God alone could, by His all-powerful will, subject two beings so different in their nature and operations to this mutual dependence. If this arbitrary and determined will of God ceased to act, this forced union would immediately terminate, just as a stone would fall to the ground when it was no longer held up in the air. Each party would recover its natural independence of the operations of the other. In this case, the soul, far from being annihilated by this disunion, which only restores it to its original state, becomes free to think independently of the body, just as I am free and at liberty to walk alone and according to my inclinations as soon as they have set me free from another to whom a superior power had bound me.

The end of this union is only deliverance and pure liberty, just as the union itself was only slavery and subjection. It is then that the soul can think independently of all the movements of the body, just as we of the Christian faith suppose that angels, who have never been confined to bodies, think in heaven. Why then should we fear this disunion, which can alone effect the entire freedom of the thoughts?

But the body itself is not annihilated; not one atom of it perishes. All that takes place in what we call death is a simple derangement of the organs; its most minute corpuscles exhale, and the whole machine is dissolved and decomposed. In whatever spot dissolution may take place, wherever accident may carry the remains of the body, not one particle ever ceases to exist. Why then should we fear that this other substance so much more noble, this thinking being that we call the soul, should be annihilated? How can we believe that the body, which cannot annihilate itself, has the power to destroy the soul that is so superior to it, a stranger to it, and absolutely independent of it? The disunion of these two beings cannot produce the destruction of either.

We readily believe that no particle of the body is lost at this separation. Why are we so eager to find reasons for believing that the soul, which is incomparably more perfect, is annihilated? It is true that God might destroy it, if He pleased, at any time, but there is no more reason for believing that He would annihilate it at the moment of its disunion with the body than during its union. What we call death being only a simple derangement of the corpuscles that form the organs, we have no right to say that this occurs in the soul precisely as in the body. The soul, which is a thinking being, has none of the properties of the body; it has neither different parts, nor figure, nor relative proportions and movements, nor change of situation. Thus, no derangement like that of the body can take place.

The soul, this thinking and willing self, is a simple being—one by itself and indivisible. There never are, in the same man, two selves or two halves of the same self. Objects are presented by different organs, producing different sensations; but all these different canals pour themselves into a common center, where they all unite.

It is this self, which is so truly one, through which each man has a true identity and is not many instead of one man. We cannot see it, hear it, or touch it. We conceive of the soul from its power of thought and will, and we perceive of the body from its extent and form. As soon as we think of the real distinction of the soul from the body, we must acknowledge that it does not possess either divisibility or form or arrangement. The body that has organs may lose the arrangement of its parts, change its form, and be decomposed, but the soul cannot lose an arrangement of parts that it has never possessed and that do not belong to it.

It may be said that the soul, being created only to be united to the body, is so connected with it that its borrowed existence ceases as soon as its association with the body terminates. But it is speaking without proof, and at random, to say that the soul is created with an existence limited to the time of its connection with the body. From whence do they draw this unreasonable conclusion, and with what right do they take it for granted instead of proving it? The body is certainly less perfect than the soul, as it is more perfect to think than not to think; we see, nevertheless, that the existence of the body is not confined to its union with the soul. After death has interrupted this connection, the body still exists in minute particles. We observe only two things: one is that the body crumbles to dust and is decomposed; this cannot happen to the soul, for it is simple, indivisible, and without arrangement of parts. The other is that the body no longer moves in dependence upon the thoughts of the soul. Ought we not to conclude on the same ground, and with more reason, that the soul also exists, and that it then begins to think, independently of the body? That the operation follows the existence is acknowledged by all philosophers. These two beings are independent of each other as much in nature as in operation; as the body does not depend upon the soul for its movements, neither does the soul require the assistance of the body for its thoughts.

It was only from circumstances that these two beings, so unlike and so independent, were subjected to acting in concert; the termination of their transient union leaves them free to operate, each one according to its own nature, which has no mutual relation to the other.

In fine, this becomes the question: Has God, who has the power to either annihilate the soul of man or continue its existence forever, willed its destruction or its preservation? There seems not the least reason for believing that He, who does not annihilate the least atom in the universe, wills the annihilation of the soul, and there is not the least appearance that such is its fate at the moment when it is separated from the body, since it is a being entirely distinct and independent. This separation being only the end of a subjection to a certain concert of operations with the body, it is manifest that it is the deliverance of the soul, and not the cause of its annihilation.

We must acknowledge, however, that we ought to believe in this annihilation that is so extraordinary and so difficult to comprehend, if God Himself has declared it in His Word. What depends only upon His arbitrary Word can be revealed to us only by Him. Those who will believe the mortality of the soul against all probability ought to prove to us that God has spoken to us to assure us of it. It is by no means necessary for us to prove that God does not will this annihilation; we are satisfied with the supposition that the soul of man, which, next to God, is the most perfect thing that we have any knowledge of, is less able to lose its existence than the mean and imperfect substances that are around it; the annihilation of the least atom is without example in the universe since the creation. We are satisfied, then, with the supposition that, as the least atom is not lost, so the soul of man is not liable to annihilation. This is the most reasonable and the most decided judgment from the first impression. It is for our adversaries to dispossess us of our conviction by clear and unquestionable proofs. These they can obtain only by a positive declaration from God Himself.

We produce the Book that bears every mark of a divine origin, for it has taught us to know and to love supremely the true God. It is this Book that speaks in the character of God when it says,

"I am that I am" (Exodus 3:14). No other book has described the Supreme Being in a manner worthy of Him. The gods of Homer subject divinity to disgrace and derision. The Book that we have in our hands, after having shown God to us as He is, teaches us the only worship that is worthy of Him. Its object is not to appease Him by the blood of victims but to lead us to love Him supremely and to prefer His will to our own, to have this love of God enter into all our virtues and eradicate every vice.

There is but one Book in the world that makes religion consist in loving God more than ourselves and in renouncing self for Him; all others that repeat this great truth are borrowed from this. All truth is taught in this fundamental truth. The Book that has disclosed to us the nature of God and the nature of man and the true worship of the heart must be divine.

Where is there another religion in which this is the great truth? Moreover, this Book, so divine in its doctrine, is full of prophecies whose accomplishment is open to the observation of the world—as the reprobation of the Jews and the admission of idolatrous nations to the true worship through the Messiah. Besides, this Book is sacred as a record of miracles performed in open day and in view of the greatest enemies to religion.

In fine, this book has done all that it says it could do. It has changed the face of the world. It has peopled the deserts with men who have been angels in mortal bodies. It has taught and cherished, even in the midst of the most corrupt and impious society, the most difficult and the gentlest virtues. It has persuaded the idolater of self to count himself as nothing and to love supremely the invisible Being. Such a book ought to be read as if it descended from heaven to the earth. It is in this Book that God has declared to us a truth that is already so rational, so probable in itself.

The same almighty and good Being, who alone could deprive us of life eternal, has here promised it to us; it is the hope of this life without end that has taught so many martyrs to despise the short and suffering life of the body. Is it not reasonable that God—who proves the virtue of every man in this short life, and who often leaves the impious in their prosperous course, while the just live and die amid suffering and obscurity—should reserve to another life the chastisement of the one and the reward of the other? This is what the sacred records teach us. Wonderful and blessed conformity between the Word of God and the truth that we bear within us! All harmonize—philosophy, the supreme authority of the promises, and this deep sentiment of truth imprinted upon our hearts.

Why is it that men are so incredulous concerning the blessed truth of their immortality? The impious declare that they are without hope and that they are, after a few days, to be swallowed up forever in the gulf of annihilation. They rejoice at it, and they triumph at their approaching extinction. They, who love themselves so madly, seem to be enamored of this horrible doctrine. They court despair. Others tell them that they have a resource in the life eternal, but they are angry at the thought; it exasperates them. They fear being convinced. They exercise all their ingenuity in caviling at these powerful proofs. They prefer perishing in the indulgence of their insensate pride and brutal passions to living eternally and submitting to be virtuous. O monstrous frenzy! Wild, absurd self-love that turns against itself and becomes its own enemy!

LETTER 42

On the True Worship of God

It appears to me that the character of true worship is not to fear God as we fear a terrible and powerful man who destroys all who resist him. The pagans offered incense and victims to certain malignant and fearful divinities to appease their wrath. This is not my idea of God. He is infinitely just and almighty, and doubtless He is to be feared, but only by those who refuse to love Him and make themselves acquainted with Him. The best fear we can have of God is the fear that we might not please Him and that we might not do His will.

The fear of punishment is useful to men who have wandered from the right path; it may restrain from crime, but it is only useful as it is the means of leading them to love Him. There is not a man in the world who desires to be feared rather than loved by his children. When we perform good actions from fear alone, we perform them merely to avoid suffering; and, of course, if we could avoid the punishment and dispense with their performance, we should do so.

There is not only no parent who would be pleased with being honored in this way, and no friend who would grant the name of friend to those who were bound to him only by such ties, but there is not even a master who would love or reward his domestics or accept their services if he saw they were bound to him by fear alone and not by any real love. With how much more reason is it that God, who has given us intelligence and affections in order that we may know and love Him, cannot be satisfied with a servile fear but desires our hearts, and that our love should return to the fountain from where it first flowed.

LETTER 43

On the Means by which Men
May Become Religious

We are too much impressed with the great disparity that exists between the grossness of the minds of most men and the grandeur of those truths that must be understood by one who would become a Christian.

What is there that sensual and evil passions have not enabled the weakest and least cultivated of men to attain? What is there that the vilest men have not invented for the perfection of the arts when avarice has excited them? What means will not a prisoner invent in his dungeon to escape from it, to obtain news of his friends, to give others intelligence of himself, or to deceive those who hold him captive? What pains would not a man take to penetrate the cause of his situation if he found himself, when he awoke from sleep, transported into a deserted and unknown island? What would he not do to discover how he had been removed during his sleep, to ascertain whether there were any vestiges of inhabitants there, to procure subsistence, to clothe and shelter his body, and to find means of returning to his own country?

Such are the natural resources of the human mind among the least cultivated men. The will is all that is essential to enable men to succeed in whatever is not absolutely impossible.

Love truth as much as you love health, vanity, freedom, pleasure, and even your fancy, and you will find it. Be as curious to know Him who made you, and to whom you owe everything, as the lowest-minded men are to satisfy their earthly desires, and you will find God and life eternal.

Let men act in this world as the one who finds himself when he awakes in a deserted and unknown island. Let men, instead of being engrossed with what they call fortune, diversions, reputation, politics, eloquence, or poetry, be occupied with answering these questions: Who am I? Where am I? Where did I come from? By whose power did I come here? Why and by whom am I created? Where am I to go to? Who are these beings around me that resemble me? Where do they come from?

Why will not men take as much pain to know themselves as Anacharsis the Scythian did to find the truth? As the Greeks did who went into Egypt, Asia, and even India to get wisdom? It requires but little light to see that we are in darkness, only a little effort to become acquainted with our own weakness; to be a true philosopher, man needs only to know his ignorance. When will men strive to develop the great mystery of their own existence? The mind of every man expands by use; it becomes elevated and enlarged in proportion to the exercise of his will and the intellectual efforts he makes. Let the soul be turned as strenuously toward good as it usually is toward evil, and you will find that the simple love of goodness will give incredible resources to the spirit in the search after truth.

If men loved truth better than themselves, as it ought to be loved, they would strive for it as earnestly as they now strive after the illusions that flatter their vanity. Love, with little intellect, will perform miracles. It is not important that uncultivated men should be able to explain with method and precision how they are persuaded in favor of virtue and religion; it is enough that they are persuaded by correct and substantial reasons, though they cannot analyze the principles on which their conviction rests or refute the subtle objections that may embarrass them.

Nothing is easier than to confuse a man of good sense with regard to the reality of his own body, although it is still impossible for him to doubt of it seriously. Tell him that the time that he calls awaking is only a time of more profound sleep than the sleep of the night; tell him that he will awake perhaps at death from the sleep of his whole life, which is only a dream, just as he thinks he awakes every morning from the dreams of the night; urge him to show you any difference that is precise and decisive between the illusion of a dream of the night, when a man is sure he is what he is not, and the illusion of the dream of a whole life. You put it out of his power to answer you, but it is not less out of his power to believe you. He will smile at your ingenuity; he feels, though he is unable to demonstrate it, that your subtle reasons have only darkened a clear truth instead of throwing light upon what was obscure.

There are a hundred examples of truths that men cannot doubt and that seem to escape them as soon as they are pressed to answer an ingenious objection to them. Truth is not the less true, and the deep conviction that all men have of it is not less a real and invincible belief, although no one has the power to explain his reasons for believing. The greatest philosophers are persuaded of a great number of truths that they cannot clearly develop or to which they cannot refute the objections.

It is very true, as some author of our time has said, that "men have not sufficient courage to follow their own reason." I am well persuaded that no man without the grace of God will, by his own natural strength, have all the constancy, all the method, all the moderation, all the distrust of himself that is necessary for the discovery even of those truths that do not require the superior light of faith. In a word, the natural philosophy that follows, without prejudice or impatience or pride, the deductions of purely human reason is a prodigy. I trust only in the grace of God to direct our reason, even within its own narrow bounds in the discovery of religion, but I believe with Saint Augustine that God endows every man with the first germ of this divine power, which imperceptibly mingles with his reason and prepares him to arrive gradually at faith. This preparation of the heart is at first the more indistinct because it is general in its effects; it is a confused sentiment of insufficiency, a desire after what we have not, a wish to find outside ourselves that which we cannot find within, a melancholy consciousness of a void in our hearts, a hunger and thirst after truth, and a sincere disposition to readily believe ourselves deceived and to think that we are in want of assistance to save us from error.

This is the secret beginning of the birth of the new man, the first springing up in the soul of that healing and free grace that gradually dissipate all darkness and conquer all the corrupt passions of man. It will be said that this is not sufficient to lead to belief in Jesus Christ, since our faith comes by our senses, and we should not have heard of the truth if the evangelists had not been sent. (See Romans 10:17.) But I maintain that if the inward dispositions answer to the grace bestowed, God will finish, by His providence, the work that His love has already commenced. (See Philippians 1:6.) He will doubtless by a miracle enlighten a man and lead him by the hand to the gospel sooner than He will let him be deprived of a light that he is worthy to receive.

A man who loves God more than himself and who forgets himself in the search after truth has already found it in his own heart. The religion of Jesus already operates within him, as it did in the hearts of just men under the ancient law—as in the descendants of Noah, in Job, and in the other worshippers of the true God. Saint Augustine was assured that Cornelius had received the Holy Spirit before he was baptized; he believed that God never abandons any but those who deserve it, that He never deprives anyone of the supreme good. He adds, in the words of the apostle, that those Gentiles who have the law written in their hearts have a part in the gospel. (See Romans 2:14–15.) You perceive that only those infidels are culpable who have received, without profiting by it, a real mercy, an offered grace, that would have enabled them to believe. It will be imputed to no one to have sinned where he had not the power to know his duty.

If we suppose the case of an infidel who faithfully uses the light of his reason, and that first germ of the grace of God implanted within him, to seek for truth with real piety, we must believe that God will not refuse the knowledge of Himself to such a man. Rather than His children should be deprived of supreme felicity that He has freely promised them, God would enlighten a man living in an unknown forest or in a desert island, either by an interior and extraordinary revelation or by sending to him teachers of His Word.

We need only bring to our minds the idea of God to be assured that He never will desert us. Will we fear that the supreme Love will cease to love? Can we believe that the infinite Good, ever pouring Himself forth on all, will deny Himself to any who are worthy of Him? Saint Augustine, on the contrary, says that God does everything to save us, except depriving us of our free will.

Whom, then, will we accuse? God, who cannot, without departing from Himself, cease to be infinitely good, compassionate, beneficent, watchful, and full of tenderness toward all His children? Or man, who, according to his own confession, is vain, stubborn, presumptuous, ungrateful, idolatrous of himself, and averse to the government of his Creator? Do not let us blaspheme against God, that we may excuse our own demerits; pride and selfishness are the causes of our errors.

God would have us love Him supremely; we must overthrow and destroy this idol of self. Jesus Christ has exterminated visible idolatry, but the idolatry within still prevails everywhere. Our reason—divested of passion, pride, and evil desires—would naturally arrive at this truth, that we have not made ourselves, and that we owe this self, which is so dear to us, to Him who gave it.

Let us add to these reflections the true idea of the Christian religion. In what does it consist? In the love of God. He wills that we should worship Him alone in our hearts. This is the true worship that the pagans never understood and that the Jews comprehended only imperfectly, although the foundation of it was laid in their own law. According to Saint Augustine, men understand the whole sense of the Scriptures as soon as they know what it is to love God; in truth, this command includes all others. The Jewish religion was only the imperfect beginning of that adoration in spirit and in truth that is the only worship worthy of the Supreme Being. Divest that religion of temporal blessings, of mysterious emblems, of ceremonies established in order to preserve the people from idolatry—in fine, of its legal policy—and the love of God alone remains. Afterward unfold and perfect this love, and you have Christianity, of which Judaism was but the germ and preparation.

IV

REFLECTIONS FOR EVERY
DAY OF THE MONTH

FIRST DAY

On the Little Faith that There Is in the World

When the Son of man cometh, shall he find faith on the earth?
—Luke 18:8

If He were to come at this moment, would He find it in us? Where is our faith? What are the proofs of it? Do we believe that this life is only a short passage to a better? Do we believe that we must suffer with Jesus before we can reign with Him? Do we look upon the world as a vain show, and death as the entrance into true happiness? Do we live by faith? Does it animate us? Do we enjoy the eternal truths that it presents to us? Do we feed our souls with them as we nourish our bodies with healthful aliment? Do we accustom ourselves to view everything with the eye of faith? Alas, instead of living by faith, we extinguish it in our souls. How can we truly believe what we profess to believe, and act as we act?

May we not fear, lest the kingdom of heaven be taken from us and given to others who will bring forth more fruit? This kingdom of heaven is faith, when it dwells and reigns in the heart. Blessed are the eyes that see this kingdom. Flesh and blood have not seen it. Earthly wisdom is blind to it. To realize its glories, we must be born again, and to do this, we must die to self.

SECOND DAY

On the Only Road to Heaven

Strive to enter in at the strait gate.
—Luke 13:24

The kingdom of heaven is entered by violence, by the strait gate, by self-denial and humiliation. The broad gate, through which we see the multitude pass, and which is ever open, leads to perdition; let us beware of entering it. We must seek the footsteps of the saints, the path worn by penitents who have climbed the precipice and gained a sure footing upon the heights by the sweat of their brows; and even then, at the very last step, it may require a violent effort to enter in at the strait gate of eternity.

It is ordained by God that we be conformed to the image of His Son, that we be crucified to self, and that we renounce sensual pleasures and submit, like Him, to suffering. But how great is our blindness! We would quit the cross that unites us to our Master. Let us live and let us die with Him who came to show us the true way to heaven. We must take up the cross if we would follow Him. We suffer in the narrow way, but we hope. We suffer, but we behold the heavens opening. We suffer, but we are willing to suffer. We love God, and His love will be our recompense.

THIRD DAY

On True Devotion

[The one who] deceiveth his own heart, this man's religion is vain.
—James 1:26

What mistakes are made about devotion! One man makes it consist in a multitude of prayers, another in a great many outward acts tending to the glory of God or the good of his neighbor. Some think it a continual desire of salvation, others an austere life. But they are all deceived if they think they have arrived at the true foundation and essential principle of piety.

Piety that is sanctified and is a true devotion to God consists in doing all His will precisely at the time, in the situation, and under the circumstances in which He has placed us. Perform as many brilliant works as you may, you will be recompensed only for having done the will of your sovereign Master. Perfect devotedness (and from this has arisen the term *devotion*) exacts not only that we do the will of God, but that we do it with love. God would have us serve Him with delight; it is our hearts that He demands of us. Such a Master is entitled to our love.

This devotion must be manifested in everything. In what contradicts our views, our inclinations, or our projects, it should make us stand ready to yield up our fortunes, our time, our liberty, our life, and our reputation to the will of God. These are the dispositions, and such will be the effects, of true devotion.

FOURTH DAY

On Weak and Imperfect Conversions

People who have lived far from God are apt to think themselves very near Him as soon as they make some steps toward Him.

Thus, polished and enlightened men make the same mistake as the peasant does who thinks he has been at court because he has seen the king. They quit their most heinous vices and adopt a rather less criminal life; but, still effeminate, worldly, and vain, they judge of themselves not by the gospel, which is the only rule they ought to follow, but by a comparison between their present life and the one they formerly led.

This is enough, they think, to canonize them; and they remain in a profound tranquility as to what is yet to be done for their salvation. Such a state is perhaps more to be feared than one of open sin, for sin might awaken conscience, and faith might revive, and they might make a great effort; but the other state only serves to stifle salutary remorse and establish a false peace in the heart that renders the evil irremediable.

These Christians are low-minded and cowardly; they would possess heaven at a low price; they do not think of what it has cost those who have obtained it; they do not consider what is due to God.

Such men are far from being converted. If the gospel had been confided to them, it would not have been what it is now; we should have had something far more pleasing to our self-love. But the gospel is immutable, and it is by that immutable gospel that we must be judged. Let us follow this sure guide and fear nothing so much as to be flattered and betrayed.

FIFTH DAY

On a Right Spirit

How much more shall your heavenly Father
give the Holy Spirit to them that ask him?
—Luke 11:13

There is no right spirit but the Spirit of God. The spirit that leads us away from the true good, however ingenious, however enticing, however able it may be to procure us perishing riches, is only a spirit of illusion and falsehood. Would we wish to be borne upon a brilliant and magnificent car if it was hurrying us into an abyss? Our souls were given us to conduct us to the true and sovereign good. There can be no right spirit but the Spirit of God; there is no other that leads us to Him.

There is a great difference between a noble, a high, and a right spirit; those may please and excite admiration, but it is only a right spirit that can save us and make us truly happy by its stability and uprightness.

Be not conformed to the world. Despise what men call *spirit*, as much as they admire it. It is their idol, but nothing is vainer. We must reject not only this false and dazzling show of spirit but also the worldly policy that has a more solemn aspect and seems more profitable. And we must enter, like little children, into the simplicity of faith, innocence of manners, a horror of sin, and a humility that is ready to take up the cross.

SIXTH DAY

On Patience in Suffering

In your patience possess ye your souls.
—Luke 21:19

The soul loses command of itself when it is impatient. However, when it submits without a murmur, it possesses itself in peace, and God is with it. To be impatient is to desire what we have not, and not to desire what we have. An impatient soul is prey to passions unrestrained, either by reason or faith. What weakness, what delusion! When we acquiesce in an evil, it is no longer such. Why make a real calamity of it by resistance? Peace does not dwell in outward things but within the soul. We may preserve it in the midst of the bitterest pain if our will remains firm and submissive. Peace in this life springs from acquiescence even in disagreeable things, not in an exemption from suffering.

SEVENTH DAY

On Submission and Conformity to the Will of God

Thy will be done in earth, as it is in heaven.
—Matthew 6:10

Nothing is done on earth or in heaven but by the will or the permission of God; yet men do not desire this will except when it promotes their own wishes.

Let us desire that His will be done, and only His, and we will make a heaven of earth. We must thank God for everything, for evil as well as good things, for evil becomes good when He sends it. We must not murmur at the conduct of His providence. We will find it is all in wisdom and adore it. O God, what do I see in the course of the stars, in the order of the seasons, but Your will, which they accomplish? Let it also be fulfilled in my soul.

Jesus said, in speaking of His heavenly Father, *"For I always do those things that please him"* (John 8:29). May we learn how far we can follow this example. He is our model, the One whose life was devotion to the will of God. May we be united to Him in this spirit. May we no longer follow our own inclinations, but may we not only pray, teach, and suffer but also eat, drink, and converse—do all things—with reference to His will. Then will our lives be a continual self-sacrifice and an incessant prayer.

EIGHTH DAY

Of the Advantages of Prayer

Pray without ceasing.
—1 Thessalonians 5:17

Such is our dependence upon God, that we ought not only to do His will, but we ought to desire to know how we can please Him. How unspeakable a happiness it is to be allowed to approach our Creator with confidence, to open our hearts to Him, and, through prayer, to hold intimate communion with Him. He invites us to pray. "Will He not," says Saint Cyprian, "grant us those blessings that He commands us to ask for?" Let us pray, then, with faith. Happy is the soul that is blessed in its prayers with the presence of God! Saint James says, *"Is any among you afflicted? let him pray"* (James 5:13). Alas, we often think this heavenly employment wearisome. The heartlessness of our prayers is the source of our other infidelities.

Ask, and it will be given to you; knock, and it will be opened; seek, and you will find. (See Matthew 7:7.) If we had only to ask for riches in order to obtain them, what eagerness, what assiduity, what perseverance we would display. If, by seeking, we could find a treasure, we would remove mountains for it. If we could, by knocking, enter into the counsels of the king or a high office, with what reiterated strokes would we make ourselves heard. What are we not willing to do for false honor? What rebuffs, what crosses, will we not endure for the phantom of worldly glory? What pains will we not take for miserable pleasures that leave only remorse in their path?

The treasure of the favor of God is the only one we cannot submit to ask for, the only one that we are discouraged from seeking. Still, to secure this, we have only to ask for it; for the word of Jesus Christ is true. It is our conduct that is unfaithful.

NINTH DAY

On Attention to the Word of God

Lord, to whom shall we go? thou hast the words of eternal life.
—John 6:68

It is to Jesus Christ that we must listen. Men must not be heard or believed, except as they speak with the truth and from the authority of Jesus. He spoke and acted so that we might attend to and study the details of His life. Mistaken creatures that we are, we follow our own fancies and neglect the words of eternal life.

We often say that we desire to know what we must do to become more virtuous; but when the Word of God teaches us, our courage fails us in the execution. We are conscious that we are not what we ought to be. We see our own wretchedness; it increases every day, and we think we have done a great deal in saying that we desire to be delivered from it. But we must count for nothing any resolution that falls short of the absolute determination to sacrifice whatever arrests us in our progress toward perfection. Let us listen to what God inspires, prove the spirit so as to know if it comes from Him, and then follow where He may lead us.

TENTH DAY

On the Right Use of Crosses

They that are Christ's have crucified the flesh
with the affections and lusts.
—Galatians 5:24

The greater our dread of crosses, the more necessary they are for us. Be not cast down when the hand of God is heavy upon you. We must measure the greatness of our evils by the violence of the remedies that the Physician of souls thinks necessary for our cure. We may make our trials a source of love and confidence and consolation, saying with the apostle, *"For our light affliction, which is but for a moment, worketh for us a far more exceeding and eternal weight of glory"* (2 Corinthians 4:17). Blessed are those who weep, who sow in tears, for they will reap, with joy ineffable, the harvest of eternal life and felicity. (See Psalm 126:5.)

Saint Paul said, "I am nailed to the cross with Jesus Christ." (See Romans 6:6, 8.) Let us pray for His spirit of love and self-renunciation. What can we suffer that He has not suffered? Weak, cowardly nature, be silent; look at your Master and be ashamed to complain. Let your love for Him reconcile you to your cross; then, though you suffer, it will be willingly.

ELEVENTH DAY

On Meekness and Humility

Learn of me; for I am meek and lowly of heart.
—Matthew 11:29

It is Jesus who gives us this lesson of meekness and humility; no other being could have taught it without our revolting at it. In all others, we find imperfection, and our pride would not fail to take advantage of it. It was necessary that He should Himself teach us, and He has condescended to teach us by His example. What high authority is this! We have only to be silent and adore, to admire, and to imitate.

The Son of God has descended upon the earth, taken upon Himself a mortal body, and expired upon the cross so that He might teach us humility. Who will not be humble now? Surely not the sinner who has merited so often, by his ingratitude, God's severest punishments. Humility is the source of all true greatness; pride is ever impatient and ready to be offended. The one who thinks nothing is due to him never thinks himself ill-treated; true meekness is not mere temperament, for this is only softness or weakness. To be *meek* toward others, we must renounce self. The Savior adds *"lowly of heart"*; this is a humility to which the will entirely consents, because it is the will of God and for His glory.

TWELFTH DAY

On the Faults of Others

Bear ye one another's burdens, and so fulfil the law of Christ.
—Galatians 6:2

Charity does not demand of us that we should not see the faults of others; we must, in that case, shut our eyes. But it commands us to avoid attending unnecessarily to them, and to be not blind to the good while we are so clear-sighted to the evil that exists. We must remember, too, God's continual kindness to the most worthless creature, and think how many causes we have to think ill of ourselves; and, finally, we must consider that charity embraces the very lowest human being. It acknowledges that in the sight of God, the contempt that we indulge for others has in its very nature a harshness and arrogance opposed to the spirit of Jesus Christ. The true Christian is not insensible to what is contemptible, but he bears with it.

Because others are weak, should we be less careful to give them their due? You who complain so much of what others make you suffer, do you think that you cause others no pain? You who are so annoyed at your neighbor's defects, are you perfect?

How astonished you would be if those whom you cavil at should make all the comments that they might upon you. But even if the whole world were to bear testimony in your favor, God, who knows all, who has seen all your faults, could confound you with a word. Does it never come into your mind to fear, lest He should demand of you why you did not exercise toward your brother a little of the mercy that He who is your master so abundantly bestows upon you?

THIRTEENTH DAY

On the One Thing Necessary

Thou art careful and troubled about many things:
but one thing is needful.
—Luke 10:41–42

We think we have many important concerns, yet we have really but one. If that is attended to, all others will be done; if that is wanting, all the rest, however successful they may seem to be, will go to ruin. Why then should we divide our hearts and our occupations? Oh, you sole business of life, henceforth you will have my undivided attention. Cheered by the presence of God, I will do at the moment, without anxiety, according to the strength that He will give me, the work that His providence assigns me. I will leave the rest; it is not my affair.

"[Father,] *I have finished the work which thou gavest me to do*" (John 17:4). Each one of us must be ready to say this on the day when we must render an account. I ought to consider the duty to which I am called each day as the work that God has given me to do, and to apply myself to it in a manner worthy of His glory—that is to say, with exactness and in peace. I must neglect nothing; I must be violent about nothing; for it is dangerous either to perform the works of God with negligence or to appropriate them to ourselves by self-love and false zeal. In that case, we act from our own individual feeling, and we do the work ill, for we get fretted and excited and think only of success. The glory of God is the pretext that covers this illusion. Self-love, under the disguise of zeal, complains and thinks itself injured if it does not succeed. Almighty God, grant me Your grace to be faithful in action and not anxious about success. My only concern is to do Your will and to lose myself in You when engaged in duty. It is for You to give to my weak efforts such fruits as You see fit—or none, if such is Your pleasure.

FOURTEENTH DAY

On a Preparation for Death

Thou fool, this night thy soul shall be required of thee: then whose shall those things be, which thou hast provided?
—Luke 12:20

Nothing is so terrible as death to those who are strongly attached to this life. It is strange that we do not form a more just judgment of the present and of the future. We are as infatuated with this world as if it were never to come to an end. The names of those who now play the most distinguished parts in life will perish with them. It is the will of God that all living things shall be swallowed in a profound oblivion, man most especially. The pyramids of Egypt still stand, while the names of those who erected them are unknown.

What then can we accomplish here? To what purpose is the happiest life, if, by a wise and Christian course, it does not conduct us to a happy death? *"Be ye also ready: for in such an hour as ye think not the Son of man cometh"* (Matthew 24:44). These words are addressed to each one of us, of whatever age and in whatever rank we may be placed. Why do we so cling to life? And why is it that we shrink so from death? It is because we do not desire the kingdom of heaven and the glories of a future world. Oh, you dull souls who cannot raise your thoughts above this world, where, by your own confession, you cannot find happiness. The true way to be ready for the last hour is to employ the present hour well and ever expect the final one.

FIFTEENTH DAY

On Our Eternal Hopes

Eye hath not seen, nor ear heard, neither have entered into the heart of man, the things which God hath prepared for them that love him.
—1 Corinthians 2:9

What a disproportion there is between what we endure here and what we hope for in heaven! The first Christians rejoiced without ceasing at the hope placed before them, for they believed that they saw the heavens opening to them. The cross, disgrace, punishment, and the cruelest death could not discourage them. They trusted in that infinite goodness that would compensate them for all their sufferings. They were transported with joy at being counted worthy to suffer; while we, cowardly spirits, cannot endure because we cannot hope. We are overwhelmed by the least sorrow and often by those troubles that spring from our own pride, imprudence, or effeminacy.

"*They that sow in tears shall reap in joy*" (Psalm 126:5). We must sow in order to reap. This life is the seedtime; we will enjoy the fruits of our labors in another. Earthly-minded men, weak and impatient as they are, want to reap before they have sown.

We desire that God would please us, that He would smooth the way that leads to Him. We are willing to serve Him if it does not cost us much. To hope for a great reward and suffer but little for it—this is what our self-love proposes. Blind as we are, will we never know that the kingdom of heaven must suffer violence, and that it is only strong and courageous souls who will be counted worthy of victory? Weep, then, since those who mourn are blessed, for God will wipe away all tears from their eyes. (See Matthew 5:4; Revelation 7:17; 21:4.)

SIXTEENTH DAY

On Our Daily Bread

Give us day by day our daily bread.
—Luke 11:3

What is this bread, O my God? It is not merely the support that Your providence supplies for the necessities of life; it is also the nourishment of truth that You dispense day by day to the soul. It is the bread of eternal life, giving us vigor and making us grow in faith. All that is within and all that is without us is bestowed by You for the advancement of our souls in a life of faith and self-renunciation. I have then only to receive this bread and to accept, in the spirit of self-sacrifice, whatever You will ordain of bitterness in my external circumstances or within my heart. For whatever happens to me each day is my daily bread, provided I receive it as from Your hands and for the support of my soul.

It is hunger that makes the food for our bodies useful and agreeable to us. Let us hunger and thirst after righteousness. The food for the mind is truth and goodness; let us seek it, feed upon it, and be strengthened by it. This is the spiritual bread of which we must eat. Let us hunger for it. Let us humbly pray to God for it. Let us be conscious of our weakness and need of it. Let us read, and let us pray, with this hunger after the food for our souls. Let us thirst after the fountain of living waters. It is only an earnest and continual desire for instruction that renders us worthy to receive these heavenly truths. To each one, this true bread of life is dispensed according to the measure of his desire for it.

SEVENTEENTH DAY

On the Peace of the Soul

Peace I leave with you, my peace I give unto you:
not as the world giveth.
—John 14:27

All men seek peace, but they do not seek it where it is to be found. The peace that the world can give is as different from that which God bestows as God is different from men. Or, rather, the world promises peace but never gives it.

It presents some passing pleasures to us, but these cost more than they are worth. It is only the religion of Jesus that can give us peace. This sets us at peace with ourselves; it subdues our passions and regulates our desires; it consoles us with the hope of everlasting good; it gives us the joy of the Holy Spirit; it enables us to be happy; it gives us peace of mind in the midst of outward trials. As the source it springs from is inexhaustible, and the recesses of the soul that it inhabits are inaccessible to the malignity of men it is to the righteous a treasure that can never fail.

True peace is the possession of the favor of God. This is found only in submission, faith, and obedience to His laws; it is the result of a pure and holy love for Him. Resign every forbidden joy; restrain every wish that is not referred to His will; banish all eager desires and all anxiety. Desire only the will of God; seek Him alone, and you will find peace; you will enjoy it in spite of the world. What is it that troubles you? Poverty, neglect, want of success, external or internal troubles? Look upon everything as being in the hands of

God and as real blessings that He bestows upon His children, of which you receive your portion. Then the world may turn its face from you, but nothing will deprive you of peace.

EIGHTEENTH DAY

On Deceitful Pleasures

I said of laughter, It is mad: and of mirth, What doeth it?
—Ecclesiastes 2:2

People of the world rejoice as the sick man does in his delirium or as those who have a pleasant dream. We attach ourselves to a shadow that flees away. We are delighted only because we are deceived.

We think we have great possessions when we are poor indeed. When we awake from the sleep of death, we will find our hands empty and will be ashamed of our joy. Woe to those who enjoy in this world a false happiness that excludes the only true felicity. Let us ever say to these vain and transitory joys, "Why do you tempt me?" Nothing is worthy of our hearts but our hope of future blessedness. All that does not rest upon this is a dream.

"Whosoever drinketh of this water shall thirst again" (John 4:13). The more we drink of the corrupt waters of the world, the more will we thirst. To the extent that we yield to evil, our hearts are dissatisfied. Avarice and ambition cause more anxiety in people for the things that they do not possess than pleasure from what they do have.

Pleasure enervates the soul, corrupts it, and renders it insatiable; the more we yield, the more we desire to yield. It is easier to preserve our hearts in a state of holiness, Christian feeling, and self-denial than to restore this state or control it when it has once gotten into the vortex of pleasure and self-indulgence.

Let us watch, then, over ourselves; let us beware of drinking of those waters that will only inflame our thirst. Let us keep our hearts with all diligence, lest the vain pleasures of the world should seduce them and leave us at last in despair at finding ourselves deceived.

NINETEENTH DAY

On Holy Tears

Blessed are they that mourn: for they shall be comforted.
—Matthew 5:4

It is the goodness of God that inspires us with the fear of losing His love, the fear of departing from the right way. This excites the tears of holy men. If we think ourselves in danger of losing what is most precious to us, we must weep. When we see only vanity and blindness, contempt and disregard of God Almighty, whom we adore, we must weep. God will not disapprove of our grief; He is the One who inspires it. Our love for Him causes our tears to flow, and He Himself will wipe them away.

TWENTIETH DAY

On Worldly Wisdom

To be carnally minded is death.
—Romans 8:6

The wisdom of the children of this world is great. Jesus Christ declares it in the gospel, and it is often greater than that of the children of light; but there is to be found in it, notwithstanding its specious and brilliant pretensions, a terrible defect. It is death to those who take it for the guide of life.

This crooked policy, fertile of inventions, is opposed entirely to that from God, which ever goes straight forward in uprightness and simplicity. Of what benefit will all their talents be to these wise men of the world if, at the last, they are caught in their own snares? The apostle Saint James calls this wisdom *"earthly, sensual, devilish"* (James 3:15). Earthly, because it limits its desires to the possession of earthly good; sensual, because it labors only for those things that flatter the passions, and plunges men into sensual delights; devilish, or diabolical, because while it has the shrewdness and penetration of a demon, it also has the malice of one. Its possessors think they deceive the whole world, but they deceive only themselves.

Blind are all those who think themselves wise and have not the wisdom that Jesus taught. They are running in profound darkness after a phantom. They are like a man in a dream who thinks he is awake and who imagines that the objects he sees are real. Thus deceived are those who are called great in the world and wise in their generation yet who are the victims of deceitful pleasures. It is only the children of God who walk in the light of pure truth.

What awaits these men who are so full of their own vain and ambitious thoughts? Often disgrace, and always death, the judgment of God, and eternity. These are the great objects that are ever before and that ever await these men, but they do not discern them. Their worldly wisdom can foresee everything except the downfall and annihilation of everything they hold dear. Deluded beings, when will you open your eyes to the light of Christianity, which will show to you the nothingness of earthly glory?

TWENTY-FIRST DAY

On Trust in God

It is better to trust in the LORD than to put confidence in man.
—Psalm 118:8

We are ever ready to confide in weak friends, and we are afraid to trust in God. We believe the promises of the world, but we cannot believe the Word of God. Let us make an effort to restore the divine order; let us confide with moderation in what depends upon ourselves, but let us set no bounds to our confidence in God. Let us repress all eagerness, all inquietude, all that we call zeal. The one who thus trusts in God becomes immovable as Mount Zion. Our trust should be more firm and elevated. *"I can do all things through Christ which strengtheneth me"* (Philippians 4:13).

TWENTY-SECOND DAY

On the Depth of the Mercy of God

Let us give ourselves to God without any reserve, and let us not be afraid; He will fill our whole hearts—these hearts that the world may intoxicate, trouble, and agitate but cannot satisfy. He will deprive us only of those things that make us unhappy. Our occupations will not be changed, but they will be performed with reference to the will of God. We will meet the approach of death in peace. It will be to us only the commencement of an immortal life. We will, as Saint Paul says, not be unclothed but be clothed, so that mortality may be swallowed up in life (see 2 Corinthians 5:4), and then we will comprehend the depth of the mercy of God.

Let us contemplate, as in the presence of God, all the proofs that we have experienced of His mercy: the light that Jesus Christ has shed upon our souls, the pure affection that He has inspired, the sins that have been forgiven us, the snares that we have escaped, the protection we have received. Let our hearts be touched with the remembrance of all these precious proofs of His goodness. Add to this the sorrows that He has sent to sanctify our hearts, for we should look upon these as proofs of His love for us. Let gratitude for the past inspire us with confidence in the future. Let us never distrust Him; let us fear only ourselves, remembering that He is the Father of mercies and the God of all consolation. He sometimes takes away His consolations from us, but His mercy ever remains.

TWENTY-THIRD DAY

On the Yoke of Jesus Christ

My yoke is easy, and my burden is light.
—Matthew 11:30

Let not the word *"yoke"* terrify us; we feel the weight of it, but we do not bear it alone. Jesus Christ will enable us to bear it. He will teach us the charm of justice and truth and the chaste delights of virtue. His religion supports man against himself and against his corrupt desires, and it makes him strong in spite of his weakness. O you of little faith, what do you fear? You suffer, but you may suffer with peace, with love for God. You must fight, but you will gain the victory. God is on your side, and He will crown you with His own hands. You weep, but He Himself will wipe away your tears.

Is it to be lamented that we are delivered from the heavy yoke of the world and have only to bear the light burden that Jesus Christ imposes? Do we fear being too free from self, from the caprices of our pride, from the violence of our passions, and from the tyranny of the world?

TWENTY-FOURTH DAY

On False Liberty

Where the spirit of the Lord is, there is liberty.
—2 Corinthians 3:17

When we obey the world, we call ourselves free because we follow our own inclinations. Foolish mistake! Is there any condition in which we do not have as many masters as we do individuals with whom we are connected? Is there any condition in which we do not depend even more upon the whims of others than upon our own? All the commerce of life is continual constraint, from the thralldom of decorum and from the necessity of pleasing others.

Besides this, our own passions are worse than the cruelest tyrants. If we obey them only in part, we must maintain a continual contest with them, and have hardly time to breathe. Then they betray us, they distract our hearts, they tread underfoot the laws of honor and reason, and they never say, "It is enough." If we yield ourselves up to them, where will they lead us? I shrink from the thought. O my God, preserve me from the fatal slavery that men madly call liberty. With You alone is freedom. It is Your truth that makes us free. To serve You is true dominion.

TWENTY-FIFTH DAY

On the Determination to Live
Entirely to God

Lord, what wilt thou have me to do?
—Acts 9:6

These were the words of Saint Paul when he was miraculously addressed by the grace of that Savior whom he had persecuted. Do we not still persecute Him by our pride and our passions? And when tribulation comes, and our pride is overthrown, and our self-love is confounded, will we not say to Him with perfect submission, "Lord, what will You have me do?"

It is not enough that this offer of ourselves is made in general terms only. It must include all the details of duty. It costs very little to desire perfection. We must truly desire it, more than all temporal blessings, even the most cherished and the most ardently pursued. We must not do less for the service of God than we have done for the world. Let us ask our hearts this question: "Am I resolved to sacrifice to God my strongest affections, my most deeply rooted habits, my predominating inclinations, and my greatest pleasures?"

TWENTY-SIXTH DAY

On the Compromises that We Would Make with God

How long halt ye between two opinions?
—1 Kings 18:21

No man can serve two masters.
—Matthew 6:24

We know that we must love and serve God if we would be saved, but we are anxious to strip His service of everything burdensome and disagreeable. We wish to serve Him if He demands only a few words and ceremonies; and these must be short, for we are soon wearied. We wish to love Him, provided we do not have to relinquish this blind love of ourselves that amounts to idolatry and that seems, instead of leading us to Him as the Being for whom we were made, to seek Him only as a resource when all other creatures fail us. We wish to love and serve Him, while we are ashamed of our love for Him, and hide it as though it were a weakness, and blush as if we were afraid and thought that He was unworthy of our love. We bestow upon Him some few of the externals of religion to avoid scandal. Thus we live under the control of the world and offer nothing to God without its permission. What sort of love and service is this?

God will enter into no other covenant with us than that in which we promise to renounce self and devote ourselves to Him, than that which is contained in the first commandment, where He exacts without any reserve all our hearts, all our minds, and all our strength. (See, for example, Deuteronomy 6:5.) If we truly love God, will we be afraid of sacrificing too much for Him? Can we love Him and be satisfied when we displease Him, or without taking pains to do His will and glorify Him, and be ever ready to testify courageously to the strength and sincerity of our love for Him?

TWENTY-SEVENTH DAY

On the Right Employment of Time

As we have therefore opportunity, let us do good.
—Galatians 6:10

The night cometh, when no man can work.
—John 9:4

Time is precious, but we do not comprehend all its value. We will know it only when it is no longer of any advantage to us. Our friends make demands upon it, as if it were nothing, and we bestow it in the same way. Often it is a burden to us. We know not what to do with it. A day will come when a single quarter of an hour may appear of more worth to us than the riches of the whole world. God, who is so free and liberal in His bounty to us in everything else, teaches us, by the wise economy of His providence, how careful we should be of the use of time, for He gives us but one instant and withdraws that as He gives us a second, while He retains the third in His own hands, leaving us in entire uncertainty whether it will ever be ours.

Time is given us to prepare for eternity, and eternity will not be too long for our regrets at the loss of time if we have misspent it. Our lives as well as our hearts belong to God; He has given them both for His service. We cannot always be doing a great work, but we can always be doing something that belongs to our condition. To be silent, to suffer, to pray when we cannot act is acceptable to God. A disappointment, a contradiction, a harsh word received and endured as in His presence is worth more than a long prayer, and we do not lose time if we bear its loss with gentleness and patience, provided the loss was inevitable and was not caused by our own fault.

Thus let us spend our days, redeeming the time, by quitting vain amusements, useless correspondences, those weak outpourings of the heart that are only modifications of self-love, and conversations that dissipate the mind and lead to no good. Thus we will find time to serve God, and there is none well employed who is not devoted to Him.

TWENTY-EIGHTH DAY

On the Presence of God

Walk before me, and be thou perfect.
—Genesis 17:1

These were the words of God to faithful Abraham. Whoever walks in Your presence, O Lord, is on the path to perfection. We never depart from this holy way unless we lose sight of You and cease to behold You in everything. Alas, where will we go when we no longer see You, You who are our light and the only goal to which our steps should tend? Having our eyes fixed on You in every step we take is our only security that we will never go astray. Faith, beaming with light amid the darkness that surrounds us, I behold You with Your look of holy love and trust, leading man to perfection. O God, I will fix my eyes on You. I will behold You in everything that is around me. The order of Your providence will arrest my attention. My heart will still see You in the midst of the busy cares of life, in all its duties and in all its concerns, for they will all be fulfilled in obedience to Your will. *"I will lift up mine eyes unto the hills, from whence cometh my help"* (Psalm 121:1).

In vain does our own foresight strive to escape the snares that surround us. Danger comes from below, but deliverance is only from on high. Temptations are without and within us. We would be lost, O Lord, without You. To You I raise my eyes, and upon You I rest my heart. My own weakness frightens me. Your all-powerful mercy will support my infirmity.

TWENTY-NINTH DAY

On the Love that God Has for Us

I have loved thee with an everlasting love.
—Jeremiah 31:3

God has not waited for us to love Him; before all time, before we were endowed with life, He thought of us and thought of doing us good. What He meditated in eternity, He has performed in time. His beneficent hand has bestowed every variety of blessings upon us; neither our unfaithfulness nor our ingratitude has dried up the fountain of His goodness to us or arrested the stream of His bounty.

O You Eternal Love who has loved me when I could neither know nor acknowledge You; immeasurable love who has made me what I am, who has given me all I possess, and who has yet promised me infinitely more! O Love, without interruption and without change, who all the bitter waters of my iniquities could not extinguish! Have I any heart, O my God, if I am not penetrated with gratitude and love for You?

THIRTIETH DAY

On the Love that We Ought to Have toward God

Whom have I in heaven but thee?
and there is none on earth that I desire beside thee.
—Psalm 73:25

We often, when we say we love God with our whole souls, utter mere words; it is a sound without any sense. We learned to speak thus in our infancy, and we continue when we grow up, without knowing what we say. To love God is to make His will ours; it is to obey faithfully His laws; it is to abhor sin. To love God is to love all that Jesus Christ loved—poverty, humiliation, and suffering; it is to hate what He hated—the vanities of the world and our own passions.

Can we think that we truly love an object that we do not wish to resemble? To love God is to hold a willing communion with Him; it is to desire to be near to Him; it is to thirst for His presence. Mankind lives in a deathlike coldness. They love a little base metal or trophy, a house, a name, an airy title, a chimera that they call "reputation." They love a conversation or a passing amusement. It is God alone whom they do not love; all our love is exhausted upon the most paltry things.

Would we not know the happiness of loving God? O God, reign in our hearts, in spite of our infidelities; let the flame of Your holy love extinguish all other.

What would we ever find truly lovely apart from You that we could not find in You, who are all perfection and the Source of every good?

THIRTY-FIRST DAY

On Love for God

God is the strength of my heart, and my portion for ever.
—Psalm 73:26

Can we know You, O my God, and not love You who surpass—in greatness, power, goodness, bounty, magnificence, all sorts of perfections, and (what is more to me) Your love for me—all that a created being can comprehend? You permit me, You command me, to love You. Should the mad passions of the world be indulged with ardor while we love You with a cold and measured love? Oh no, my God; let not the profane be stronger than the divine love.

Send Your Spirit into my heart; it is open to You, and all its recesses are known to You. You know how far it is capable of loving You. Weak and helpless being that I am, I can give only my love. Increase it, almighty God, and render it more worthy of You.

V

SHORT MEDITATIONS ON DIFFERENT SUBJECTS TAKEN FROM THE HOLY SCRIPTURES

FIRST MEDITATION

Lord, to whom shall we go? thou hast the words of eternal life.
—John 6:68

We do not understand the gospel; we do not comprehend its instructions; we do not penetrate its spirit. We are very curious about the teachings of men, but we neglect those of God. One word from the gospel is worth all the other books in the world; this is the source of all truth.

With what love, what faith, what adoration ought we to listen to the words of Jesus Christ! Henceforth let us say to Him, with Saint Peter, *"Lord, to whom shall we go?"* A single moment of self-communion, of love, and of the presence of God will enable us to perceive and understand the truth better than all the reasonings of men.

SECOND MEDITATION

Take heed, therefore, that the light which is in thee be not darkness.
—Luke 11:35

It is not surprising that our sins should be displeasing in the sight of God; but the fact that imperfections grow even out of our virtues should make us tremble. Our wisdom is often only a worldly and selfish policy; our modesty is a composed and hypocritical exterior to attract praise and for the sake of appearance; our zeal is an effect of fancy or pride; our frankness is only thoughtlessness; and so on.

How do we shrink from those sacrifices that we make to God while they appear so meritorious in the eyes of the world! Let us beware, lest our light turn into darkness.

THIRD MEDITATION

Love not the world, neither the things that are in the world.
—1 John 2:15

We rail at the world, but we carry the world in our hearts. The world is that multitude of people who love themselves and who love the creatures of earth without reference to the Creator.

We are then the world ourselves, since it means only those who love themselves and who seek in created things the felicity found only in God. We must confess, then, that we are of the world and that we have not the spirit of Jesus Christ.

It is shameful to renounce the world in appearance and to retain its principles—jealousy of authority, love of reputation that we do not merit, dissipation in company, anxiety for all those indulgences that flatter the senses, cowardice in the exercise of Christian duties, a disinclination for the study of the truths of the gospel. This is the world; it dwells within us, and we love it, while we are so anxious for its favor and so apprehensive lest it should forget us. Happy was the holy apostle to whom the world was crucified and who was crucified to the world! (See Galatians 6:14.)

FOURTH MEDITATION

My peace I give unto you: not as the world giveth.
—John 14:27

It is sacrificing little to relinquish this phantom called the world; they are to be pitied who think they lose much in quitting it. Every true Christian renounces it. It is to seek a sheltering port from the storm.

The world, it is true, promises peace, but it never gives it. It yields us some fleeting pleasures, but they cost us more than they are worth. It is the religion of Jesus alone that can give peace to man. It unites him with his Savior, it subdues his passions, it controls his desires, it consoles him with the love of Christ, and it gives him joy even in sorrow. And this is a joy that cannot be taken away.

FIFTH MEDITATION

See that ye love one another with a pure heart fervently.
—1 Peter 1:22

The apostle teaches us in these words that our charity should lead us to be always attentive not to give pain to our neighbor. Without this watchfulness, charity, which droops in the world, would soon die. A word uttered with haughtiness or unkindness may overcome a weak spirit. Being so dear to God, the friends of Jesus should be treated by us with gentleness. If we neglect this carefulness, we are deficient in charity.

We are always attentive to those who are dear to us, and this watchful love should fill our hearts. *"Feed my sheep"* (John 21:16, 17). These words of Jesus are applicable to us all as an exhortation to cordiality and tenderness toward one another.

SIXTH MEDITATION

The Son of man came not to be ministered unto, but to minister.
—Matthew 20:28

This is what everyone should say who has any authority over others. It is a ministry. We must truly serve those whom we appear to command; we must bear with their imperfections, correct them with gentleness and patience, and lead them in the way to heaven.

We must be all things to all men; consider ourselves as made for them; soften, by our humility, the most necessary reproofs; never be discouraged; and ask God to give that change of heart that we cannot produce by our efforts.

Let us examine ourselves in relation to those who are committed to our care and for whom we are accountable to God.

SEVENTH MEDITATION

Learn of me; for I am meek and lowly in heart.
—Matthew 11:29

Only the Son of God could have given us this divine lesson. What has He not done for the love of us? What has He not suffered? What does He not still feel for us? He was led like a victim to the slaughter, and no one heard Him complain; yet we complain at the slightest evils; we are sensitive, irritable, and proud.

There is no true and constant gentleness without humility; while we are so fond of ourselves, we are easily offended with others. Let us be persuaded that nothing is due to us, and then nothing will disturb us. Let us often think of our own infirmities, and we will become indulgent toward those of others. Let us apply to our hearts these sublime and touching words of the Son of God, *"Learn of me; for I am meek and lowly in heart."*

EIGHTH MEDITATION

Whosoever exalteth himself shall be abased;
and he that humbleth himself shall be exalted.
—Luke 14:11

Do we desire glory? Let us seek it in its true place; let us seek that which will endure forever. O noble ambition, to dwell eternally with the Son of God! But how weak, how childish, this eager desire for distinction in the world—for a name, a reputation, more evanescent than the vapor that is the sport of the winds! Is a vain show worth so much pain?

Let us aspire after true greatness, which is found only in humility. God rebukes the proud even in this world, and in the world to come, they are abased; but the humble, even in this life, will receive the respect that they have not sought and eternal glory will be the recompense of their contempt of false and perishing honors.

NINTH MEDITATION

I sleep, but my heart waketh.
—Song of Solomon 5:2

We sleep in peace in the arms of God when we yield ourselves up to His providence in a delightful consciousness of His tender mercies—no more restless uncertainties, no more anxious desires, no more impatience at the place we are in. For it is God who has put us there and who holds us in His arms. Can we be unsafe where He has placed us and where He watches over us as a parent watches a child? This confiding repose, in which earthly care sleeps, is the true vigilance of the heart. Yielding itself up to God, with no other support than Him, it thus watches while we sleep. This is the love of Him that will not sleep even in death.

TENTH MEDITATION

Lord, teach us to pray.
—Luke 11:1

Lord, I know not what I ought to ask of You; You love me better than I can love myself. O my Father, give to Your child that which he knows not how to ask. I dare not pray either for crosses or consolations; I present myself before You. I open my heart to You. Behold those shortcomings in me that I know not myself. See and do according to Your tender mercy.

I adore Your will without knowing it. I am silent before You; I yield myself up; I would sacrifice myself to Your will. I would have no other desire than to do it. Teach me to pray; pray Yourself in me.

ELEVENTH MEDITATION

Yea, Lord; thou knowest that I love thee.
—John 21:15

Saint Peter said this to our Lord, but will we dare to say it? Can we love Him of whom we do not think? What friend do we have of whom we would rather not speak? Where are we more wearied than at the foot of His altar? What do we do to please our Master and to render ourselves what He wishes us to be? What do we do for His glory? What have we sacrificed to Him? Do we prefer Him even to our lowest interests, to our most unworthy pleasures? Where, then, is our love for Him?

Unhappy, however, are those who do not love the Lord Jesus, who has so loved us. If we do love Him, can we be insensible to all His benefits? *"Neither death, nor life, nor angels, nor principalities, nor powers, nor things present, nor things to come, nor height, nor depth, nor any other creature, shall be able to separate us from the love of God, which is in Christ Jesus our Lord"* (Romans 8:38–39).

TWELFTH MEDITATION

The LORD is my shepherd; I shall not want....He leadeth me beside the still waters.
—Psalm 23:1–2

How weak it is in us to seek anything but God! While we have the Source of all good, we think ourselves poor. We desire to find, even in piety, earthly consolations. We look upon it rather as a softener of the ills that we must endure than as a state of renunciation and sacrifice of self. From this arise our discouragements. Let us begin by yielding ourselves up to the will of God. When serving Him, let us have no anxiety about what He will do for us. A little more or a little less suffering in this short life will be of little consequence.

What can I want if God is with me? Yes, God Himself! He is the infinite and the only good. Vanish, all you false goods of earth, unworthy of the name you bear, that often only make men wicked. God alone is good, who always dwells in my soul. Let Him deprive me of my pleasures—riches, honor, power, friends, health, and even life; if He does not estrange Himself from my heart, I will still be rich; I will have lost nothing; I will have preserved my all.

The Lord has sought me in my wanderings, has loved me when I have not loved Him, and has regarded me with compassion, notwithstanding my ingratitude. I am in His hands; I feel my weakness and His strength with such a support that I will want nothing.

THIRTEENTH MEDITATION

Learn of me; for I am meek and lowly in heart:
and ye shall find rest unto your souls.
—Matthew 11:29

Almighty God, I come to be instructed at Your feet. You are present, and You call me by Your tender mercies. Speak, Lord, for Your servant hears. O Eternal Majesty, I come before You to receive everything I desire from You and to renounce myself without reserve.

Send me Your Holy Spirit, O my God; let Him become mine. I would open my heart to this Spirit of love and truth; let Him enlighten me and teach me to be meek and lowly. O Jesus, it is You who have given me this lesson of gentleness and humility. You teach me to find in it rest for my soul. Alas, how far I have been from finding this peace! I have sought it in the vain imaginations of pride, but pride is incompatible with peace; it ever desires what it does not possess; it wishes to pass for what it is not. It ever exalts itself, and God continually resists it by the envy and contradictions it meets in the world, or by its own imperfections, which it cannot help feeling. Unhappy pride can never know the peace of the children of God, who are meek and lowly of heart.

FOURTEENTH MEDITATION

The LORD gave, and the LORD hath taken away.
—Job 1:21

This, O Lord, is what Your servant Job said in the excess of his sufferings. It is Your mercy that has put these precious words into the heart and lips of a sinner like me. You gave me health, and I forgot You; You deprive me of it, and I return to You. Blessed be God who has taken away His gifts to bring me to Himself.

O Lord, deprive me of all else, but restore to me Yourself. All of Yours are Yours. You are the Lord. Take from me riches, honor, health, and everything that would separate me from You.

FIFTEENTH MEDITATION

Whether we live therefore, or die, we are the Lord's.
—Romans 14:8

O my God, what is death or life to me? Life is nothing; it is even a snare if it be too dear to me. Death can only destroy this house of clay; it delivers the soul from the contamination of the body and from its own pride. It frees it from the influence of the tempter and introduces it forever into the kingdom of truth.

I ask not, then, O my Father, for health or for life. I make an offering to You of all my days. You have counted them. I would know nothing more. All I ask is to die rather than live as I have lived, and if it is Your will that I depart, let me die in patience and love. Almighty God, who holds the keys of the tomb in Your hand, to open and close it at Your will, give me not life if I will love it too well. Living or dying, I would be Yours.

GENERAL PRAYER

O God so great, yet so intimately with us, so far above these heavens, and yet so near to the lowest of Your creatures, filling immensity and yet dwelling in the bottom of my heart, so terrible and yet so worthy of love—when will Your children cease to be ignorant of You? Oh, that I might find a voice loud enough to reproach the world for its blindness and to declare with authority all that You are. When we tell men to seek You in their own hearts, it is easier for them to seek You in the most distant parts of the world. What is more unknown and more remote from vain and dissipated men than their own hearts? Do they know what it is to enter into themselves? Have they ever sought the way? Can they imagine what it is, this inward sanctuary, this impenetrable depth of the soul, where You will be worshipped in spirit and in truth? They dwell far off in the objects of their ambition and their vain pleasures.

Alas, how will they listen to heavenly truths, since, as Jesus Christ has said, they do not regard even earthly truth? As for me, O my Creator, shutting my eyes to external things, which are only vanity and vexation of spirit, I would commune with You in my secret heart through Your Son Jesus Christ.

O God, we do not know You. It is by You that we live, that we think, that we enjoy; and we forget the Source of all things. We see nothing but through You, the universal light; by You alone do we see anything, and yet we do not see You. It is You who gives all—to the stars their light, to the fountains their waters and their courses, to the earth its plants, to the fruits their flavor, to the flowers their splendor and their perfume, to all nature its abundance and its beauty. To man You give health and reason; You give him all things. You do all and rule over all. I see only You. All other things are but as shadows before the eyes of him who has once seen You. And the world does not see You! But alas, the one who has not seen You has seen nothing; he has passed his life in the illusion of a dream. He is as if he were not—more unhappy still, for, as I learn from Your Word, it would have been better for him if he had not been born.

O God, when will we return love for love? When will we seek the One who always seeks us and whose arms are always around us? It is in Your paternal bosom that we forget You. The blessings we every moment receive from You, instead of touching our hearts, turn our thoughts away from You. You are the Source of all happiness, and Your creatures are only the channels through which it flows. And the stream leads us away from the fountain. This boundless love follows us everywhere, and we flee from it. It is everywhere, and we do not perceive it. We think ourselves alone when we are only with God. He does all for us, and we do not trust in Him. We despair when we have no other resource than His providence, and count for nothing infinite love and infinite power.

EVENING PRAYER

O Lord, watch over me, lest I sleep the sleep of death. Alas, this day—has it not been void of good works? In it we might have gained everlasting life, and we have lost it in vain pleasures. Perhaps it may be the last of a life undeserving of Your mercy. O fool, perhaps this very night Jesus may come to demand of you your soul, the image of the great God, which you disfigured by sin.

O Lord, grant that while I sleep, Your love may watch over me and keep guard around my heart. I am the prodigal son; I have wandered far away into a strange land where I have lost all my inheritance. Here I have fed with the vilest and the grossest animals. I am starving and a beggar, but I know what I will do. I will return to my Father. I will say to Him, "O my Father, I have sinned against heaven and against You. Are You not the good shepherd who leaves His flock to go into the desert after a single wandering sheep? Have You not declared that there is joy in heaven over a single sinner who repents? You will not then despise a humble and contrite heart."

O Lord, watch over my spirit while I wake and my body while I sleep, that I may sleep in peace and awake in Jesus. Pity my weakness. Send Your holy angels, spirits of light, so that they may keep far from me the spirit of evil that is ever around me. Grant that I may resist it with the courage of faith.

Give penitence to sinners, perseverance to the just, and peace to the dead. Let my evening prayer rise to You, O Lord, and let Your blessing descend upon me.

ABOUT THE AUTHOR

François de Salignac de la Mothe-Fénelon (1651–1715) was a French archbishop, theologian, and writer whose excursions into the contemplative life, especially the quietism espoused by Madame Guyon, caused controversy in the church of his day. His writings remain, though, as an encouragement and source of spiritual growth for many Christians today.

Fénelon, descended from a long line of nobility, started his higher studies in 1672 at Saint Sulpice seminary in Paris. He was ordained a priest in 1676 and appointed director of Nouvelles Catholiques ("New Catholics"), a college for women who taught converts from French Protestantism. Fénelon, while never supportive of Protestantism, was nonetheless critical of harsh treatment toward Huguenots (French Protestants) and the many forced conversions that occurred under King Louis XIV. Fénelon instead held open meetings with Protestants to share the Catholic doctrine in a nonthreatening environment.

Fénelon's first important work, *Traité de l'éducation des filles* (*Treatise on the Education of Girls*), was conservative overall but also suggested noncoercive concepts for educating females that were very innovative for his day. His second and best-known work, *Les Aventures de Télémaque* (*The Adventures of Telemachus*), outlined Fénelon's political beliefs through the account of Telemachus's search for Ulysses. It was written during Fénelon's time as tutor to Louis, Duke de Bourgogne, the grandson and heir to Louis XIV.